MW01231869

EAST OF LOS ANGELES

EAST OF LOS ANGELES

SHAWN KHALIFA

Copyright © 2016 by Shawn Khalifa

All rights reserved. No part of this book may be reproduced, stored, or transmitted by any means—whether auditory, graphic, mechanical, or electronic—without written permission of both publisher and author, except in the case of brief excerpts used in critical articles and reviews. Unauthorized reproduction of any part of this work is illegal and punishable by law.

This is a work of fiction. Names, characters, places, and incidents either are the product of the author's imagination or are used fictitiously, and any resemblance to actual persons, living or dead, business establishments, events, or locales is entirely coincidental. The publisher does not have any control over and does not assume any responsibility for author or third-party websites or their content.

ISBN-13:978-1-523-47877-4

THANK YOU GOD!

This book is dedicated to my Mother and my Sister.

A World without Hope,
    Is a World without Jesus!

                    -Author

New York City, 2016

New York City-2016

Nobody knew it would be like this. On such a beautiful
New Years Eve in Times Square. The snow fell lightly on five
million happy American shoulders. The most to ever grace these
streets at one time. The mad Republican Eileen O'Conner was defeated
in this years November Presidential election. She was now at
her Orange County, California home in retreat from the public
eye after the nations first Mexican American President elect
Juan Carlos beat her in a landslide victory for the Democratic
Party.

It is now 11:15p.m. in Times Square amd president Carlos
was to begin his speech to the nation at 11:20p.m. from his senate
seat state of Utah. The Salt Lake City crowd of 300,000 that
he stood infront of was hardly comparable to the five million
who braved the crowded Manhattan streets centering around Times
Squre. The only thing that the two crowds had in common was the
light snow that fell on them.

First lady Jeniffer Carlos stood beside her husband whispering
in his ear, "Go get em baby, I love you."

President Carlos flashed his perfect smile at her as he
strode to the podium, graciously waving to millions of Americans
who chose to watch their future leader this New Years Eve. Nobody
knew it would be like this.

After Lady Gaga's performance finished the Presidents
face appeared on all of the screens in Times Squre. The crowd
loudy cheered as it took the President five minutes of "Thank
You's" to quite them down. Times Square has never had a quite
moment in the minutes leading up to the ball drop. Never until
this one.

"My fellow Americans. As we approach the new year in a

few short minutes, we have a historic year ahead of us. We are
no longer going to be the police of the world. Today's world
is too small for us and those other powers that wish to see us
fail as a nation. The United States interest no longer exist
ouside of our shores. It's time for us to do our nation building
in our own nation. Skid Row needs hope, the 9th ward needs to
float, and the South Side of Chicago needs to be the best side
of Chicago! I will....," as President Carlos began his next
sentence a bullet from a high powered rifle entered the top of
his skull exploding his brain as his body thrust to the floor
violently. The Secret Service did not think to watch out for
one of their own hovering above in a Secret Service helicopter
where they assumed the assassin had destroyed his target from.

As the nation gasped as a whole, the Presidents live
assassination became the least of their worries for at 11:30p.m.
the stealth Chinese made gas bombs began hitting the largest
cities of the United States. Eleven year old Jackson was excited
to see the sky light up as he watched the snow fall on Times square.
Jackson just thought it was part of the celebration. He knew
different when the pellets came down emitting gas. Millions of
people fell around him as if going to sleep where they stood
and then falling. He knew they were not sleeping because nobody
was breathing, except him! Nobody knew it would be like this.

Chapter-1

16-years Earlier (2000)

"Stop it Champ!" Champs mother yelled at him as he climbed from the back seat of her Honda Civic to the front passenger seat.

"Mom, I just wanted to grab my toy." Champ whined back to his mother as he took a seat with a Stone Cold Steve Austin action figure in his hand. Stone Cold Steve Austin was Champs favorite WWF Super Star. He would never have let his friends from 60th street in South Central Los Angeles know he played with action figures.

"See Champ, I fucking told you not to climb over the seats while I'm driving!" The Red and Blue lights of the Los Angeles County Sheriff's Deputies car flashed in Linda's rearview mirror as she drove east on the 60 freeway.

She pulled over to the side of the freeway. "You can get hurt or anything and now I got to hear it from this stupid ass Cop and get a fucking ticket. Put on your damn seat belt!"

Champ did as his mother demanded and a few tears came

down his face as he realized that he had gotten his mother in trouble.

"Ma'am you need to keep that child in his seat." The officer stated when he got to Linda's drivers side window.

"I know officer I love my boy, and am going to make sure he stay's in his seat."

"That's great ma'am," The officer said sarcastically. "But I still need to write you this ticket."

"Fine!" Linda said. She retrieved her drivers license and registration for the officer.

After seeing Linda's I.D. the officer looked at her strange and asked, "Is your husband Ky Washington?"

Linda was bothered by the officer asking about her ex-husband. "He's not my husband anymore." Linda stated proudly.

"Yeah I remeber Ky when I used to work the Twin Towers, (Part of the Los Angeles county jail system) he had pictures of you." The officer spoke. Excited for some reason.

"Oh, were you the one who tore his pictures up and left them in the toilet?" Linda retorted as she reached out to grab her ticket.

The officer did not respond. After handing Linda her ticket the officer returned to his vehicle and watched Linda drive off.

*

Champ was the only child of Ky Washington and Linda. Ky moved with his parents from Detroit to Los Angeles in 1976 when Ky was just 14-years old. Ky's Somali mother married his Black

American father in the year they first met in 1961. A year later
Ky was born. Getting to know the local teen's in Watts was tuff
at first for Ky. He had friends he met at school who belonged
to a Blood gang. They played on the football team at their middle
school. Ky was already a big 14-year old at 6'2 180 pounds. He
didn't have a problem with bullies. Ky's problem was more political
than that. Ky's mother was more then familure with clan warfare
in her native Somalia. She just could not understand why it was
happening here in America.

The Project's (or P.J.'s as they are better known) where
Ky lived was dominated by a Crip gang. Ky being friends with
their rival Blood's could have gotten his whole family murdered.
That soon changed when Ky made friends with the kid's in his
Project's and became a member of the Crip's. His former friends
had become his most hated enemies. In the 9th grade at just 15-
years old Ky shot to death one of his old football teammates
outside of their high school for throwing up the 'B' (For Bloods)
gang sign at him.

In juvenile court Ky was sentenced to California's Youth
Authority until he reached the age of 25. After being released
from the Youth Authority the 6'5 225 pound Ky met Linda Evans.
One year later at the age of 26 his one and only son was born
to the beautiful 24-year old Linda.

Linda's life was much simpler than Ky's. She grew up in
Torrance California with middle class white parents. At the age
of 23 Linda got a job with an engineering company in Inglewood.
That was the same year that she met the charming Ky Washington.
He had this glow about him that drove her 5'10 140-pound body
crazy. She could see past his gang tattoos to his heart. He needed
to be loved and she saw herself as just the right White woman
to give it to him.

Ky and Linda bought a house in South Central Los Angeles
on 60th street. Linda had become a lead engineer with her company

bringing in a good $63,000 a year while Ky traveled 80-miles
East of Los Angeles every morning to Perris California where
he sold Marijuana in the Jarvis street apartments (or locally
known as The Jay's). On a good day Ky brought home $1,200. On
a bad day Ky would bring home no less than $450. More money than
his wife made or more money than he could ever make from a legal
job. His job site was staffed 24-hours a day 7-day's a week by
Crip's and Blood's from Compton and Watts. The local gang's in
Perris were too young and well outgunned to ever mount a resistance
to these Los Angeles foreigners who were sucking up most of the
drug money to be had in this City.

Champs parents spoiled him buying him the best of everything.
They should have bought him a safer place to live.

It wasn't until now when champ was 12-years old that his
mother was finally doing that. That's why they were now driving
East on the 60 freeway out of Los Angeles.

4-years prior when Champ was just 8-years old his father
was implicated in the shooting death of a liquor store clerk
around the corner from their home in South Central. Nobody in
the neighborhood thought that Ky did it. Even a few local hood's
knew who did it. It wasn't Ky. The L.A.P.D. could care less who
did it as long as they were Black, belonged to a gang, or had
a criminal record. Those were the 3-strikes against Ky that cost
him his freedom.

In 1997 after a year of fighting his case from the Los
Angeles County Jail Ky was convicted of 1st. degree murder, plus
the enhancement of robbery. After being sentenced to Life in
Prison Without the Possibility of Parole Linda filed for her
divorce.

A 4-year stint as a single White mother raising her Black
child in South Central Los Angeles was all Linda could take.
Linda heard the horror stories from the neighborhood and work

alike. Mothers had their son's thrown in jail for mudering some
other mothers child. Family homes being shot to bit's and the
youngest of children were normally the victim. Linda's co-worker
Janice just buried her second son in 3-months.

*

For years before and to come mothers were doing the same
thing as Linda. Moving East of Los Angeles to the Inland Empire
(known as The I.E.). Made up of Riverside and San Bernardino
counties the Inland Empire offered safer affordable housing while
at the same time allowing parents to keep their job's in Los
Angeles. Safer did not always equal safe when moving to a poor
area in one of the Inland Empires many cities.

While driving East on the 60 freeway the smog got worse
as Linda drove through the city of Riverside. The young Champ
was asleep in the passenger seat of the red Honda Civic. Getting
on the 215 South Linda got an excited feeling as she passed the
city of Moreno Valley and then the March Air Reserve Base. There
it was. The sign that once welcomed her now ex-husband on his
way to work every morning. The sign now welcomed Linda and her
charming 12-year old son to the promise of a better life with
a new start.

The large sign perched on the side of the 215 freeway
read; "Welcome to the city of Perris''The place for Business."

Ky alway's told Linda of how nice it was out here. They
could get a place for a quarter of what they paid in Los Angeles.
Linda was not ready to comitt to a long commute to work at that
time but now the time was right. The place may have just been
a little wrong. She had no way to know it. Nowhere could be a
worse place for her son to grow up than South Central Los Angeles.

The Honda Civic got off of the freeway at D street in
downtown Perris. Linda liked the feel of this place. When Linda

was a teenager her parents had drove her passed Perris on their way
to San Diego. It has grown quite a bit since that time with all
of the new suburban type track homes built in uptown. There was
not even an uptown Perris when she passed through here then. As
Linda exited the freeway onto the over 100-year old D street
she looked up at the looming castle like mansion set on top of
a hill to her right. Something told her in her heart that she
was ment to be here with her son.

Champ woke up in time to see the castle as they passed
by it. "Cool mom is that where we live!" Champ said this excited
but already knowing that wasn't their home.

"Yeah that's our house baby boy." Linda innocently lying
to Champ with a smile.

"Good now all we need is a helicopter so we can get here
faster. That was a long drive mom." Champ yawned as he said this.

"Are you hungry?" Mom asked

"Really hungry! I want a burger." Son hungered.

"Well let's see what they have here." Linda said as she
turned off of the historic D street and onto 4th street.

4th street was a commercial area with lot's of businesses
and places to shop and eat.

Champ spotted a Jack in the Box and pointed, "There mom
let's get some Jack in the Box!"

"Sounds good to me." Linda entered the drive thru.

When Linda pulled up to the window to pick up their milk
shakes and burgers she noticed the normal glass window that slid
all of the way open to exchange money than food. In South Central

there was double bullit proof exchange windows. When one opened
the other closed to keep you from sticking a gun through the
window to comitt a drive thru robbery.

When Linda pulled infront of her apartment on 6th street
she couldn't figure out where to park. There was an older skinny
Black woman with graying hair standing infront of the 4-apartment
structure. She wore small shorts with a black dusty tank top
ᴸ(it had white stains on it) revealing her boney arms and legs.

"Excuse me ah ma'am, we are trying to figure out where
we should park? We just moved in to an apartment here." Linda
asked the dusty woman.

"Oh hey yall live here now, I'm Carrol! I live in apartment
1." Carrol approached the red Honda Civic as she said this.

Champ had a miserable look on his face almost throwing
up his half eaten cheese burger when Carrol put her hands on
the roof of the car and bent down to speak with them through
the open front passenger side window. Champ did not know which
smell was worse, Was it her rotted teeth breath or graying under
arm hair? Champ put the rest of his burger in the brown paper
bag and set it on the floor next to his Stone Cold action figure.

"Oow you so cute!" Carrol reached in to pinch Champs cheek.

"Hi Carrol we just moved into apartment 4." Before Linda
could finish speaking Carrol keeping her right hand on the car
pointed with her left, "Y'alls live right down there in the back!
See right there!"

"I know Carrol!" Linda getting impatient said, "Where
can we park at because there is no spot's left on the street?"

"Oh you got's to go to F street an turn down the alley.
It's some spot's back there."

"Alright Carrol thanks very much."

"A handsome you goin eat the rest of that burger you put on the floor down there?"

Champ handed Carrol the bag but refused to speak to this woman. He felt if he breathed to hard he might die.

"You's a shy baby," Carrol winked at Champ as she backed away from the car with the bag in her long fingered hands.

Champ felt he'd rather suffocate than let that lady touch him again.

Linda drove around back to the alley where there was a place to park, right by the door to their apartment.

"This is it, Champ are you ready?"

"Hell yeah!" Said Champ picking up Stone Cold. Champ rushed to his new front door. Champ was excited about it being a two story apartment. His mother already told him it was smaller than the house they left behind on 60th street in South L.A., but the upstairs part made the apartment sound exciting.

When Linda put the key in the door to unlock it she thought to herself, "60th street L.A. now 6th street Perris. Look's similar to one another but 6th street  is quieter."

The door opened to their living room. Furniture was already in place. The stairs were to their right running along the wall. Champ was up the stairs in a flash. Upstairs was a small area with 4-doors in pairs on two different wall's. The smaller bedrooms on one side, one bathroom, one master bedroom on the other.

Champ checked the first door infront of him. Empty bedroom. The door next to it opened revealing all of Champs stuff. Champ put Stone Cold on his bed and looked outside of his 2nd story window. Below he saw a closet sized back porch. Behind it he saw a small house that reminded him of his old house on 60th street.

Downstairs of the apartment held a small living room, space for a small dinning table, small kitchen, sliding glass door leading to the small back porch. One closet, one restroom. It was more than enough for Linda and her son.

For the first night since they could remember they went to sleep without hearing gunshots, or sirens.

*

East of Los Angeles wasn't such a bad place. The commute to work was going to take some getting used to, but one of Linda's good friends from work was going to take the trip with her during the weekdays. That would make living 80-miles from work a bit more doable.

Linda thought about her ex-husband Ky. He had always wanted to make this move with his wife. Get out of the city and move to the suburbs. If Ky would have known that the L.A.P.D. was out to get him, he would have demanded they move."At least they're safe now." Ky thought to himself from prison knowing they finally made the move to Perris.

Linda had yet to send her new address to her ex-husband who was in Pelican Bay State Prison. She would because even though she refused to be married to a prisoner she would always have love for Ky. He would always be the father of her precious son.

*

On the opposite side of Perris in what was called Uptown lived one of Linda's coworkers who made the move from Los Angeles years earlier. In 1992 Colleen Atkif moved her two young children from a small apartment in the Jungles to a nice two story track home. The Jungles are a run-down part of Baldwin Hills in Los Angeles that had yet to recover from riot's, and violent drug gangs who murder each other in broad daylight. Colleen's Perris neighborhood started out as the ideal place to live but over the years became known as Ashbury Hell when the local gang's matured.

Colleen was also a single mother trying to raise a 12-year old son named Shawn, plus a 17-year old daughter named Jennifer. Colleen was a White woman who married a charming Egyptian man named Hamdi Atkif. Their marriage fell apart when Hamdi got into drug's and began repeatedly going to prison.

Linda and Colleen were good friends. They now carpooled to work every morning Monday's through Friday's. They left Perris at 4:30a.m., and didn't get home until 4:30p.m.. From Perris to Inglewood. Then back to Perris.

Champ met Shawn on his first weekend in Perris when Linda went to Colleen's house for a Saturday night dinner. Colleen's home was triple the size of Linda's apartment.

It was the last week of November in the year 2000 when this dinner took place. Champ turned 12 on November 3rd, and Shawn on November 16th. The duo was ripe for getting into trouble. Shawn asked his mom if he could go around the Block with Champ to introduce him to the kid's around the neighborhood. Colleen said that she didn't care but it was up to Linda. Linda did not mind as long as they returned within the hour.

The kids agreed to be back in a hour then they both left the house. Jennifer went to her room to study. The 17-year old was do to graduate in 2001. She craved getting stright A's working very hard to achieve it. Jennifer had big plans for her life but she was worried about her little brother. She could remeber like yesterday the day he was born. Jennifer was only 5-years old but her mother Colleen let her name the little guy. She picked Shawn. Not because the name was particularly special to her but because 3-kid's in her classroom were named Shawn.

Now that Shawn was 12 he was getting into trouble at his middle school. She knew he was smoking weed. Shawn's eye's were always red when he came home from school, or after ditching pretending to come home from school. No matter how much Jennifer complained to their mother, "Mom! Shawn's been smoking pot! Look at his eye's, smell his breath!"

When Colleen first walked in the door she was too tired after long day's of work to yell at her son. She would calmly tell him, "Shawn you better not be smoking pot, let me smell your breath."

"Mom Jenny's lying, here smell my breath." Shawn would blow in his mothers face.

After smelling colleen would look sad at her daughter, "Jenny I don't smell anything. Stop yelling at me and leave your brother alone."

Jennifer would give one last hopeless look at Shawn. "Shawn tell her!"

Shawn would give his evil smile. "Tell her what Jen? You're crazy!"

Truthfully Shawn was high as a kite everyday.

*

Linda was 36-years old, and colleen was 51. They could have been sisters for all that they had in common. Right now their biggest focus in life was on their son's. Colleen didn't have to stress over her 17-year old stright A daughter. If she wasn't doing her studying right now she would be having a long distance phone call with her 22-year old college boyfriend who lived in Utah. Her love. Juan Carlos.

*

The sun was barely setting and it was a chilly 58 degrees when Champ and Shawn left the house. Champ had on a black and red pair of Jordans on his feet, black jeans, blue Dodgers jacket with a blue L.A. Dodgers hat. Shawn wore his normal swat-meet clothes. Blue jeans, black sweater, gloves, and beanie.

"A man so you was living in L.A.?" Shawn asked Champ.

"Yeah man, it was crazy out there! My friends were getting killed, or locked up everyday!"

"It's cool you came out here, there's alot of dude's that moved from L.A. to Perris." They were walking around the corner to a local area known as The Block.

The Block was basically a East-West street meets a North-South street that both ended were the other one started. A better name for it should have been the turn.

"You know anybody out here from 60th street?" Champ asked.

"Naw, but it's a dude in the next block from Main Street, A bunch of people from Compton in the Jay's, and 3 from 40th street that live on 5th street downtown. Oh and my homeboy and his brothers came out here from the P.J.'s in Watts."

"What's the name of the one's on 5th street?"

"I only know Damen. He's 13. The other two are in their 20's."

"I know Damen!" Champ said.

"Yeah he's cool! I hang out with him sometimes." Replied Shawn.

"He wasn't cool when he left South Central!" Champ stated with a; I wouldn't be hanging out with him if I were you, look on his face.

"What he do out there?" Shawn questioned

"He got locked up with his homeboy in L.P. juvenile hall but his homie got 12-years and he got out."

"He told on him?" Shawn asked.

"That's what his homie said. I want to holler at him though. You said he live's on 5th street?"

"Yeah, you'll catch him hanging out at the 5th street apartments."

"Cool I'll go over there. What's 6th street like anyway's?" Champ asked wanting to know more about his new street.

"It's cool but I don't go over there that much because they got the 6th Street Crips. Lazy and his brother are crazy! It's about 20 of them over there. The 6th streets don't like people who live over here where I'm at. Watch out for 7th street P-13's!"

"What's a P-13?"

"That's the Mexicans from Perris Trece, they will shoot you just because you're black."

"Sounds like home." Spoke Champ.

"Some of them can be cool but most of them are racist as fuck." Said Shawn.

"Do you bang?" Champ asking Shawn if he was a gang member.

"No! I get along with almost everybody, what about you?"

"All of my friends in L.A. are gang members, I just always wanted something more for myself." Said Champ thinking about how sad he would make his mother if he joined a gang. It would probably kill her he feared.

Champ and Shawn arrived to a house party on The Block. Champ had a bad feeling about this.

Chapter-2


    At a one story house the garage was open with a large
number of young black men enjoying themselves. From the house
to the street directly infront of it, everybody was smoking or
had a 40oz in their hand. Like they told Champ when he walked
up with Shawn to Cottons car, (Cotton was the neighborhood celebrity
rapper, about 10-people circled the open drivers side door of
his green Bently) "This is a hood party, who the fuck is you?"

    Everybody eyeballed Champ as Bad News (Cottons brother)
confronted him. Lucky for Champ Shawn spoke up for him, "Ah he's
cool News, that's my homey, he just moved out here from the city!"

    "Oh you with Shawn, we ain't trippin on you then!" Bad
News, and everybody else went back to paying attention to Cotton.

    "I got that new C.D. done. Neighborhood Watch, you all
goin get a copy!" Cotton pushed his C.D. into his car's C.D.
player. Champ and everybody else listened.

"I'm stright from Perris nigga, and I like to blast on trigga's,
and I'm small but I'm getting bigga, everyday, everyday...

East side of my city on the wild west coast,
Uptown 5150 my homies doing the most,
Growing up with gang sign's showing N.P.M.,
Joke's getting popped I don't want to be them,
No fear on my block Cuz in Cali we active,
Mead Valley is actors,
Don't react all they do is act fuck ya phony ass,
Y'all don't put in work,
Throw on my ski mask an watch your bodies jerk,
Y'all nothing your turf is made of dirt,
God don't even love you, you have no worth,
Clicked up with little kid's we finna take um off the Earth,
Cotton is back better hold on to your purse...

And who said Mead Valley was gangster's,
Riding the Perris Loc's dick you bitches is prankster's,
Fucking with the east side of Perris we Hoodster's
P.L. killa that's just my nature...

The hardest one's from Perris Loc's is Little Money and Wigi,
Real respect real them cuz-in's can see me,
My hood's in the city your's is in the outskirts,
We fitted with N.C. jerseys y'all wear gold skirts,
You carry hunting knifes we carry pistols,
I got a big cannon hit it's target like a missile,
Y'all roll with the P.P.D., not the P.M.V.,
They shut you down like AIDS do your whole body,
I'm in your barrio,
Running up on you slow,
Shutting down your show,
Cuz it's 2001 and you bitches got to go..."

Everybody applauded Cottons work in their own special
thug way. Shawn waved Champ to come over to the house with him.

They went into the garage and Shawn told Champ that he could
wait for him on the vacant spot on the couch, next to a 16 year
old hood-rat named Angel.

Before Shawn entered the house he told Champ, "A homey
I know that girl is pretty but don't let her get you, her name
is Angel and she fuck's everybody, then their daddy's, then their
gran-daddy's."

Champ laughed when Shawn said this but Shawn didn't smile.
"Seriously homey! She'll give you something."

"Okay, okay yeah I got you! I ain't fucking with her."
Champ went and sat on the couch in the garage as Shawn entered
the house.

Angel looked at Champ as soon as he sat down. She liked
what she saw in the youngster. "You want to hit this?" Angel
was handing Champ a blunt.

"Ah naw I don't smoke." Champ said letting his eye's drift
up and down this sexy Puerto Rican girl's figure. If her skirt
was any shorter he could tell you what color panties she had
on. If she was even wearing any?

"What kind of guy are you, You don't smoke?" Angel let
the smoke slowly drift from her mouth to Champs face.

"Damn girl what the hell is wrong with you! I told you
I don't smoke!" Champ leaned back to get his face away from the
smoke. Champ jumped to his feet sideways bumping into one of
the gang members Tantrum. The unexpected bump caused Tantrum
to drop his almost empty 211 40oz.

"Cuz, what the fuck!" The 19 year old Tantrum pulled out
his 9mm hand gun as he spun around to face the dumb mothafucka
that pushed him.

"I'm sorry man, I was," Champ was cut off.

"Nigga who is you Cuz?" Tantrum growled at Champ while holding the pistol to his right cheek staring him in the eye's.

"I don't know that nigga Cuz! Smoke um Cuz! That nigga's a Perris Loc!" Were all chant's from behind Tantrum. Perris Loc was all Tantrum needed to hear. He hated them filthy no good Perris Jokes.

"**Boom!**" Was the last thing the 12 year old Champ heard as he fell backwards in what seemed like slow motion. Champ saw the gun flash four more times as he hit the floor and instict told him to try and crawl backwards. Champs sound was gone but his eye's stayed open. His face was burning as well as his chest and hand. Champ wondered if his face was still there? He could now hear faintly. He was being dragged. Somewhere? They had a hold of his arms. Champs eye's were closing. He was going to sleep for good. He was being taken so that his killers could finish the job. Champ did not want to be awake for that! He stopped fighting the sleep. He welcomed it...

*

"Boom!" Champ shot up to a seated position in a hospital bed. The gun shot he heard inside of his head woke him. An instant pain he felt in his face made him cry out and bring his right arm up to his face. The cast on his right hand didn't make his hand any softer as it came into contact with the bandage on his right cheek.

"Baby calm down everything's alright now Champ, I'm here for you, mama's here for you baby!" Linda's tears fell off of her face as she rushed to her son's bedside to comfort him.

When Shawn came running into his house looking terrified without Champ at his side Linda's heart sank. "Cha Cha Champ got shot! He need's help!" Every word Shawn spit out was like a butcher knife ripping in and out of Linda's heart.

"Where is my son! Where is my baby!" Linda yelled at Shawn with a haunting scream. Shawn ran from the house and Linda ran behind him to the block.

No mother deserves to see their child dead in the street. Brutally gunned down in cold blood. That is exactly how Champ looked to his mother. His arm's were raised above his head as if freezing so he would not be shot. She didn't know that his arm's were like that only because that is how he was dragged and left to die in the street. His blood trail from where he had been shot to where he now lay had been calmly washed away with a water hose. Nobody was going to tell. The local police will rule it off as just another gang related drive-by shooting.

Champ and his mother were equally excited about Champ surviving the shooting. The most noticeable scar was from where one bullet passed through Champs cheek. The single bullet to the chest missed Champs heart but punctured his right lung. One bullet to his right hand and two to his right thigh rounded out his wounds. Champ needed surgery to remove the bullet's from his chest and thigh. The bullet's bullet's went through his cheek and hand. Champ was shot five times on his first weekend in Perris.

*

Rules were set in place for Champ. As soon as he was healthy enough to go to school he would only be able to leave the house for that reason. The weekends would become Linda and Champs time to hang out, go to Perris lake to swim, Perris High School to swim in the summer. Champs favorite adventure was their trip

to Oceanside. He loved the beach and was getting good at boogie
boarding.

Champs middle school was a mile and a half from home.
Champs mom was gone to work by the time he got up every morning,
but lucky for him he alway's had a breakfast waiting for him
in the microwave. All Champ had to do was warm his food up. On
his walk to school Champ would avoid going down 7th street. He
would walk West up 6th street until getting to A street. South
at the end of A street was Champs middle school.

After the shooting Champ became less sociable and failed
to make any friends in his neighborhood. At school Champ was
getting stright A's with no distractions. That soon changed when
8th grade started.

*

The young Champ was soon to turn 14 years old when he
started the 8th grade. In his 3rd and 4th period classes was
a 13 year old Mexican girl named Sofia. Since first sight Champ
could not stop thinking about this girl. It took Champ two weeks
to work up enough courage to speak to her. Champ fell in love
with Sofia before they had even exchanged their first words.
When they finally did Champ was certain she was the only girl
he ever wanted to fall in love with and he was only 13 years
old. From the day they started speaking they began walking to
and from school together. Sofia lived on 7th street. Her over
protective brother Eddie was a senior at Perris high school.
He used to drive her to and from school until she started walking
with Champ. Eddie was more into God than gang's so he never hung
out with the gang members that plagued his street. Because Champ
had to go to Sofia's house to walk with her to school Champ now

walked down 7th street everyday with no problems. No problems until.

A flirtatious whistle could be heard from the front of one of the houses Champ and Sofia walked passed on their way to school. It was March of 2003 and the now 14 year old Champ had been walking down 7th street for the past 7 months with no problems. "Why now?" He thought to himself.

"A Sofia!" A Mexican voice called out from the porch of a home that they had just walked passed.

When Sofia stopped to turn and see who called her name the voice spoke again, "I see you got jungle fever A!".

Sofia's face turned flush red and she turned back to walking towards school. Champ put his arm around her saying, "Just ignore them Sofia they're shitheads."

"Why are you with that Myate homes?" The voice spoke again and Champ could feel his anger rising. He just had to stay calm or he was going to turn around, run over and punch the dumb **bastard** who was talking shit. The empty beer bottle that was thrown at them was all it took.

Champ took his arm from around Sofia and went storming to the man's house. Champ dropped his backpack to the ground.

"No Champ! Come on let's go to school!" Sofia tried to hold onto Champs arm but he was too strong.

"Come out to the street and see me if you're so bad!" Champ yelled at the man while standing infront of his house.

Macho was a 38 year old high ranking member of the P-13's. He had no time to fight a 14 year old black kid in the street. Then again he didn't have to. He had people for that. With another whistle (this one more of a code than flirtatious) younger P-13's withen earshot began coming from backyards, down the street, and from other houses. Withen a minute eighteen P-13 gang members began to form a circle around Champ.

Champs emotions went from angery to slightly frightened. He looked passed the people around him for a brief second. Where the hell was Sofia at? Champ lost track of his 5'2 Angel. His mind went back to the guy's around him. They all taunted Champ with racial slurs provoking him to fight. Champ put his fist up as a sign of defiance. The gang members laughed at him for doing this. Macho put his hand up so his homey's would quiet down. Than he began speaking.

\*

The P-13's were not the only one's to hear Macho's whistle. Over on 6th street Lazy and his brother Bone from the 6th street Crip's were sitting inside of Lazy's gray Buick. Lazy sitting in the drivers seat just lit up a Newport cigarette dipped in Shirm. They had the windows rolled down because hot boxing Shirm would be fatal. Lazy had a 38 revolver filled with six hollow tip bullet's on his lap. He kept extra bullet's in his pocket. Bone had a sawed-off shotgun on his lap. When the lighters flame hit the Shirm stick the whole thing ignited but Lazy expertly blew on it to leave only the cherry burning. That did not stop Bone from yelling, "Put it out nigga, put it out, blow on it!"

"Shut the fuck up Bone I got this shit!"

"You ain't got shit nigga you almost blew the car up!"

"I'm about to blow you up." Lazy picked up his gun while

hitting the Shirm stick then passed it to his brother.

"Aw yeah I'm finna get wet nigga!" Bone said as he took a hit from the stick.

"If some police roll up on us today they finna get murdered nigga!" Lazy said as he got the stick back from his brother to take another hit.

"Yo, don't even talk about the police. I'll blast myself before I go to jail for this shit." Bone gripped the sawed-off shotgun on his lap.

"A nigga pass me that shit back!" Bone said.

"Shut the fuck up nigga!" Lazy yelled holding the Shirm stick down by his knee while looking stright ahead as if looking at something.

"Let me get the..."

"Shhhh!" Lazy quieted his brother. Looking over to Bone he said, "Did you hear that?"

"Hear what nigga give me the stick!" Bone grabbed the Shirm stick from his brother.

"Bone I heard them Mexicans nigga, I think they out to get us?" Lazy leaned forward and started the Buick.

Bone looked at his brother crazy, "You high nigga! I don't see no Mexico's around here!"

Than a troubling thought hit Lazy. Maybe the S.A.'s had caught one of their homey's and he was in trouble? Lazy was going to find out. He put the car in drive and turned left on Perris Boulevard. Stopping on 7th street they seen it to their left.

"Is that the homey right there?" Lazy asked his brother.

"Naw he dont look like the homey, he's a brotha though."
Then it hit Bone. "Oh that's that little nigga that stay over
there by Carrol an them. He got that white mama."

"You still be fucking old crack headed Carrol?" Lazy asked.

"Naw man you know I ain't fuck that old bitch! I just
be over there serving that's all!"

"That ain't what she said nigga. She came by the spot
one day and said, 'where that nigga Bone at? He said he was going
to give me some more dick, that's goin be my baby's daddy!" Lazy
teased his brother.

"Shut up nigga pussy is pussy, you'd probably fuck too
if she let you!"

Lazy shook his head at that thought and said, "Hell naw!
You's a nasty motha fucka nigga!"


*


Macho began trying to talk some Mexican sense into Champ.
"We see you walk down our street everyday homes, we don't say
anything to you, now you come to my house and disrespect me in
my own barrio, come on now A, you gotta get punished for that."

"Look, I don't even know you guy's I just want to get
to school." Champ wanted to walk away but his path was blocked.

"Oh you want to go to school, why didn't you just say

so, and here I was thinking you wanted to fight me." Macho said
with a grin that soon faded away to an angry mad dog. "You think
I'm fucking stupid bitch, Chubby take this fucking Myate to school!"

Chubby pulled out a mini sword looking knife. "No problem
ese!" As he stalked toward the shaking Champ.

Champ jumped backwards as the knife came towards his gut,
narrowly missing him.

"Oh you want to make this fun!" Chubby stated as he brought
the knife back to strike again. This time somebody punched Champ
in the back of his head as the knife came. As Champ leaned forward
from the punch his left forearm made contact with Chubby's blade.
Champ let out a scream of pain just as Chubby punched Champ square
in the face. Champ fell to his back. Champ was now stretched
out on the street. Ironically this is what was to save Champs
life.

*

Lazy and Bone had been watching the confrontation as the
gray Buick sat idle on Perris Boulevard. Car's honked then drove
around them on this busy street. The Shirm had them too high
to care.

"A nigga you want to help him out?" Lazy asked.

"I don't give a fuck about him, but I would like to shoot
one of those beaners." Was Bone's response.

"Shit me too Cuz!"

"You want to walk over there?" Bone asked.

"Shit I feel like I can fly more than I can walk right now nigga."

"Drive up then." Bone said.

"You drive nigga!" Lazy said from the drivers seat.

"Cuz it's your car!"

"What do I do?" Asked Lazy forgetting how to operate his motor vehicle.

"Take your foot off the motha fucking brake nigga!"

Lazy took his foot off of the brake and the Buick started to roll forward. "Turn nigga turn!"

Bone reached over to the car's steering wheel and turned it left onto 7th Street towards the crowd of Mexican's. The brothers were so high Lazy forgot about his gas pedal. The car slowly coasted toward the group standing in the street. The gray Buick was about 50 yards away from the group when they started paying attention to it.

Macho retreated to his porch when he noticed Lazy and Bone cruising torwards them at lower than low speed. The Blacks stayed off of 7th Street and the Mexicans off of 6th. That's how it went to keep the peace. Macho waited by his front door and watched. If need be he could run to his living room, knock the cushions from the sofa and retrieve his fully automatic M-16.

"Watch me nigga, I'm goin do this!" Bone told his brother while stepping out of the moving car. Bone felt like Superman. The Shirm had control of his mind and body.

"Where you going nigga don't leave me!" Lazy opened his door getting ready to jump out and run toward Macho while shooting

his 38 revolver at him. Lazy hated all Mexicans but he hated
Macho more. Before Lazy could jump out of the car his brother
rolled onto the moving car's hood with his sawed-off shotgun.

"Awww nigga I'm King Kong!" Bone yelled out as he stood
on the hood of the Buick facing the Mexicans. "Boom!" The shotgun
came to life dropping three Mexicans while the other one's ran.

Lazy leaving the car rolling with his brother on the hood
ran forward while drifting to the left at the same time. Lazy
emptied all six shot's at Macho then stumbled over a curb falling
on his face.

Macho dodged the volley of bullets that sped at him by
diving through his half open front door. The windows in Macho's
living room shattered and chips of wood fell from his door. Macho
was angry.

Lazy stood up with a busted lip holding onto his empty
gun. Seeing his brother surfing down the street on his car Lazy
ran to catch up.

When the shooting started Champ managed to crawl behind
a parked car. As soon as Lazy and Bone were passed him Champ
darted for Perris Boulevard where he ducked left running up the
alley between 7th and 8th until reaching A Street.

Macho burst out of his front door. From his porch he unloaded
a full clip from his M-16 at Lazy.

Lazy dove head first into the open drivers side door of
his rolling car. His face planted onto the passenger seat. Bone
laid down on the hood as the M-16's bullets ripped into the Buick's
frame and windows. Bone's right shoulder blew up as a round from
the M-16 left a gaping hole where his joint socket used to be.
Muscle and tissue held his arm to his body. The sawed-off shotgun
flew to the street.

Lazy sat up when the shooting ceased and his driving skills came back. Lazy hit the gas pedal and made a sharp left turn on F Street tossing his brother off of the hood of the car.

Bone didn't know he was shot. The shirm kept him from feeling the pain. When Lazy made the sharp turn Bone knew something was wrong when his right arm didn't work to hold on. Falling to the street Bone hit his head hard but popped up in a flash. Bone's right arm dangled as he opened the passenger side door with his left arm. Bone took his seat inside of the car.

On A Street running to his middle school Champ held the bottom of his shirt to the wound on his forearm.

"Champ oh my God!" Sofia saw Champ run by her as she hid in the bushes of the 13th Street Park. Sofia was scared and crying. She worried about Champ but did not know how to get him help. All she could do was hide in the park and cry.

Champ heard her and stopped to see her running towards him. His nose bled with his arm. "Oh my God we have to get you help! The school has a nurse let's go!" Sofia took off running towards the school with Champ.

"Are you okay Sofia?"

"Yes I was just scared I had to take off. I didn't know what to do Champ?"

"You did the right thing Sofia. All I cared about was you."

Sofia loved the injured Champ caring about her more than himself. She wanted to spend the rest of her life with this boy and she was only 13.

Chapter-3

15-Miles North of D Street...
March Air Reserve Base...
Riverside California...

After the terrorist attacks of 9/11 the United States
government began get smart polices which funded various high
tech defense tool's for the NSA, FBI, CIA, and the Secret Service.
The top hundred most threatened cities in the United States also
received special funding to creat specialized police units. These
units could be activated and used at the discretion of the
aforementioned government agencies when ever the need arose.

The CIA received a special project known to the few who
knew of it's existence as 'Trump Card'. Trump Card referred to
a top secret satellite that recorded high resolution images of
Earth 24 hours a day 7 day's a week. What made this satellite
special was it's ability to think for itself. Unknown to us
hundreds of Trump Cards now monitor the United States as well
as 48 other nations.

Wherever a gun fired in the satellite's assigned location it zoomed in on the incident and recorded. If a group of 10 or more suddenly gather Trump Card will watch them. Something as simple as a child's birthday party can trigger the sensitive camera on the satellite. As soon as Trump Card assesses the event as unimportant it will back off and go back to watching everybody. The infrared camera could do the U.S. census bureau job for them in minutes. The entire population of Los Angeles County could be counted in under 5 minutes. Nothing is left private. Every cold gun is revealed, 80% of the murders in South Central could be solved, night looks just like day to Trump Card.

This is why the technology is so secret that only a handful of CIA know about it. And only one person in the White House.

The CIA's purpose for Trump Card is not to stop crime in the United States. It is to stop another 9/11 from ever occurring again. There were 5 Trump Cards alone watching the major counties of Southern California. Los Angeles, Orange, San Diego, San Bernardino, and Riverside all had a Trump Card assigned to them.

The Trump Card over Riverside was being monitored at a state of the art underground CIA bunker under the March Air Reserve Base.

Located adjacent the 215 freeway (between the tri-city area of Perris, Riverside, and Moreno Valley) the former active Air Force Base was now used to transport military equipment all around the world with it's large military cargo planes.

The CIA had at it's disposal two predator drones that were stationed at March. The five person CIA team assigned to the bunker often took the drones on test flights all over Southern California to pass time.

Only two of the CIA operatives had high enough security

clearance to know about Trump card, or access to the Red Room.
The Red Room required not only one pass code to enter but also
a retinal scan, hand print, then a second pass code. Once inside
of the Red Room the room did it's own scan to make sure only
approved personnel was in the room.

Agents with the highest clearance had a small micro chip
the size of a grain of sand injected into their left hand between
thumb and index finger. Once the Red Room secured it's nuclear
blast resistant doors, the high tech computers came on. Agent
Brian Benson and Samuel Richardson first worked together on a
special opp's team in Afghanistan. The 26 year old Brian was
a member of the CIA for 3 years when he was assigned to join
a Navy SEAL team during the invasion of Afghanistan in 2001.
29 year old Samuel "Ryder" Richardson was also a member of the
CIA assigned to SEAL Team 4. Both Brian and Samuel held Red Room
clearance. The 6'1 205 pound Brian and 6'3 220 pound Samuel were
born fighters. Their high I.Q. also made them ideal CIA operatives.

*

September 2001...

Two Stealth helicopters flew into a rough valley of the
Kandahar Province. The target. Osama Bin Ladin. The world watched
with America the burning brought to Manhattan as two large passenger
planes flew dramatically into the World Trade Centers iconic
towers. Thousands of innocent people lost their lives. OBL would
become the face of the horrific attack. Good intel placed him
inside of a cave near the location where the helicopters sat
down.

18 SEAL team members filed from the first helicopter while
16 SEAL team members with the two CIA operatives departed the
second. Everybody was well versed to their mission. Secure the

purported mastermind of the September 11 attacks and bring him
back alive to the secret CIA base in Pakistan. The United States
Government had plans for Afghanistan. They needed the leader
of al-Qaeda alive. The invasion was set to begin in a few short
hours and the last thing the Government wanted was their reason
for being there killed on the first night.

It was a slaughter from the time the first bullet was
fired. The 75 man al-Qaeda team protecting the cave could not
see the SEAL's through the darkness. All they could do was fire
wildly at the muzzle flashes.

The SEAL's night vision helped them pick off the insurgents
one after one. The SEAL team from the first helicopter stormed
one of the two entrances of the cave while Samuel led the second
team into the other one. The cave had many dip's and turns. After
dropping another 30 insurgents the two teams met inside of the
cave. There was one tunnel deep inside of the cave left to clear.
Samuel led both teams in. They SEAL's surrounded a bearded man
assumed to be Osama Bin Ladin who was praying on a very large
prayer rug.

Samuel put two darts in the man's back knocking him unconscious
The unconscious body of OBL was loaded into helicopter 2 with
the two CIA operatives and 10 SEAL's. The other helicopter loaded
injured SEAL's and the rest of the team flying them to an Aircraft
Carrier in the Indian Ocean. Helicopter 2 flew to the CIA base
in Pakistan. Once at the base the two CIA operatives exited the
helicopter with Osama. The helicopter then flew the SEAL's to
the Aircraft Carrier to rejoin their counterparts.

The Caucasian Brian and African American Samuel were covered
from head to toe as to not reveal a hint of their identity when
the mark regained consciousness. Osama Bin Ladin awoke to find
himself tied to a metal chair with a black hood covering his
head. Samuel and Brian stood silent guard inside of the interrogation
room. One on each side of the door in a perfect position for

Osama to view them when his hood was removed. Instead of M-16's
the masked Samuel and Brian now held Chinese made assault rifles
with the Chinese flag clearly visable on their uniforms.

The CIA often played by the motto of no rules. Deception
was fair game. Two Chinese Americans walked into the interigation
room speaking Mandarin Chinese. Agent Kim and Cho were both members
of the CIA. Osama was now fidgeting in the chair. The black hood
was removed.

Speaking in Arabic Cho began, "You are in great danger.
The Americans are soon to invade Afghanistan. The Chinese Government
believes you to be an asset to us. That is why we saved you before
the Americans could murder you."

Osama knew the Chinese did not like him so he had trouble
believing this man. Was this really the Chinese? Maybe this was
the Russians or Americans playing mind games with him? He had
helped coordinate several terrorist attacks in China. They were
carried out by terrorist groups in western China that were loyal
to al-Qaeda. What did the Chinese want with him if not to kill
him?

It was Kim's turn in Arabic she said, "We are willing
to free you here in Pakistan but we need you to understand our
purpose. We have never trusted the Americans enough to care about
their well being, but what we do care about is China. If you
agree to use your influence to stop attacks on Chinese interest
and soil we will free you. If not then we will turn you over
to the Americans. If you go back on your agreement in the future
and we can link a terrorist act in our nation to you, then we
will be back to get you again but this time it will be to deliver
you to the Americans as a token of our peoples good will. They
will toture you more than we could ever dream of. Keeping you
alive for years with a daily torture routine for breakfast."

Osama was not in a position to negotiate terms. He agreed

to the offer. Osama had no plans to uphold the agreement once
in the safety of his own people. The Americans knew this but
they did not care. In ten years they were going to come get this
man again. Only murdering him that time. His body would have
to be dumped into the ocean to cover up the listening and tracking
device that was going to be planted surgically into his left
eardrum. The device would work for a length of 20 years or longer
but the Americans would not need it to work that long. Their
project only had a time table of ten years to complete. Their
cover of bombing  caves was perfect for digging the tunnels
necessary for the top secret project of building nuclear missile
silos. The Americans would easily shoot down Russian and Chinese
satilites in the area simply telling their respective Governments
it was a security threat to the U.S. troops on the ground. Instead
of militarily the Russians and Chinese would retaliate with votes
at the U.N.. The U.S. felt it was a fair trade.

Osama was hooded, injected, implanted, then left at an
abandon house in Paskistan. When he awoke he would step out of
the house to find himself in a familure area quickly getting
back into the political game. The bug in Osama's ear would help
foil terrorist plots in the future as well as aid in the capture
of high ranking al-Qaeda members for the next ten years. The
CIA was good at it's job.

*

Agents Benson and Richerdson proved their vaule to the
Agency and were both rewarded with the "Trump Card" job at March.
Samuel Richerdson was in charge with Brian Benson as his second
in command. Agents Kyle Pollard, Marcus Johnson, and Kim Bryant
also were assigned to March. They mainly worked standard satellite
images from terrorist hot spots, flew Predator Drones in CIA
missions and provided intelligence support for agents in the
field.

While Samuel had a wife and kid's at home in a big house in the hill's of Lake Elsinore, Brian preferred his single lifestyle. Brian was a 24 hour 7 day's a week type of Agent. When he did have a little down time he would often spend it with the very attractive Kim Bryant. Kim was a 5'7 swimmer at U.C.L.A. and top of her class at everything else. After 4 years at U.C.L.A. she was recruited by the Agnecy.

Brian and Kim worked the night shift from 6p.m. to 6a.m. mainly working their Somali mission with field Agent Ron Davis. Ron was deep cover acting as a member of a Somali war clan. His misston was a long term one where he was to move up in the clan's rank's and monitor the deals and going on's this clan made with Yemen, al-Qaeda, and more importantly China. The mission was in it's infant stage and the 21 year old Ron was a simple foot soldier often in harms way. Eventually another agent would join Ron as a member of the clan. Right now it was baby steps and they needed to see how Ron would fare in this deadly mission.

From 6a.m. to 6p.m. the bunker base at March was run by Samuel, with the assistance of Agents Pollard and Johnson ages 26-28 respectively. March was a new young base for the CIA run by new young operatives but it was none the less important. Even though Brian had an apartment next to March in Moreno Valley he often slept at the bunker itself.

The Sun had just come up in the month of March 2003 and Samuel arrived to the bunker with two cup's of Starbucks coffee. One for him one for Brian who would be in the Red Room working with Trump Card.

Through the night Brian had been scaning the hot spots around Riverside County. With Trump Card the Agent had learned about how a Mexican drug cartel moved it's drugs to a drop house on 7th Street in downtown Perris. From the drop house the drugs would be taken to it's distributer in Los Angeles. After the Mexican drug cartel sold the drugs to the different gang's in

Los Angeles they were distributed throughout the entire country.
The Black gang's brought the drugs back into the Inland Empire
through a distrabution system that worked magically out of Moreno
Valley.

Brian had given the Moreno Valley Police Department a
few anonymous tip's in the past about suspicious 18 wheelers
traveling down Alassandro Boulevard. They local police uncovered
large amounts of Marijuana and Cocaine. It was not Brian's job
to stop the drug trade so he nolonger gave tip's and the drugs
kept flowing.

This past night at two in the morning he watched a pimp
murder one of his prostitutes on University Avenue in Riverside.
The pimp would get away with the murder for lack of witnesses.
Two young Hispanic males in a brown car dumped a dead body on
Day Street in Edgemont. The young Black male lay lifeless. The
Police would find his deceased body but no leads as to who left
him there.

Brian watched hundreds of crimes he witnessed through
Trump Card go unpunished. He wanted to do something, solve some
murders, robberies, rapes, but he couldn't. Trump Card didn't
exist.

"What's up Bry, how are things looking this morning?"
Samuel entered the Red Room handing Brian a cup of coffee then
taking his seat.

"Things are smooth on the T.C. Caught a hooker murder
early with a body dump a little later, you know the normal stuff.
No bombs anywhere in the County. We're pretty safe."

"Hey um, what's going on with your guy in the Horn?" Samuel
was referring to Agent Ron Davis mission in Somalia.

"Actually things are going really well Sam."

"Oh I'm glad to hear that. How is the Clan taking to him?"

"They love him like a brother. They went off the coast yesterday and hijacked an Australian cargo ship."

"Really? What did the Australian's do?"

"Wired a hefty 12 million dollar ransom to the Clan. Our man's turning out to be pretty valuable to them."

"I see! Any news on the Ethiopians possible invasion?"

"The Pentagon has images that the Ethiopians may be getting ready to go in this week. Their going to try and end some of the Clan wars, but I can see them losing more than they can gain. We're keeping Ron well informed of the situation."

"Good, well I'm going to catch up on my guy in Iran." Samuel rolled his chair to a conference screen where he would be briefed on an Agent who was posing as a member of Iran's Revolutionary Guard. The operation was being ran by the CIA base in Dallas. Samuel was supervising the operation.

*

Being away from his family for long hours put a strain on Samuel's marrage to his beautiful Black wife Lisa. With no emergancies Sam could get home by 6:30p.m. in time to eat dinner with his wife and two daughters. His oldest was 9, the other one 6. They loved their daddy and were heartbroken at least two nights a week when his dinner plate would go cold. Arriving too late or not at all.

Sometimes in his spare time Samuel would watch his family with Trump Card. His wife would drop the girl's off at school.

Lisa would get to work right on time at her dental practice in Temecula. When Samuel couldn't get to one of 9 year old Jasmin's soccer games he watched on Trump Card.

Samuel told his daughter of how special she was. How he would always be watching over her even when she could not see him. Jasmin didn't by it, and told her daddy she needed him at her games. She felt it made her play better when her daddy could cheer her on. Samuel promised his daughter he would never miss one of her games. But he already did she believed.

Today Samuel wanted to make a point of checking on his wife Lisa. He suspected she was cheating on him and he wanted to know if it was true.

Early that March morning Trump Card zoomed in to a group of people gathering on 7th Street in downtown Perris. "Hey Sam we got some guy's grouping up infront of that drop house I told you about on 7th Street."

"The one the Tijuana cartel uses?" Samuel asked still curious even knowing this wasn't their job. Their job was to make sure no unauthorized explosives were in Riverside County. Once some were detected a team was sent to secure them, and whomever was in possession. Samuel had many contact's in Washington and the Pentagon. He felt one day he could persuade higher up's to let the FBI, or Secret Service use Trump Card to solve crimes, or even protect the President. Until then it just wasn't his job.

"Yeah the one with that gang banger Macho living in it. You think the local police would be smarter." Brian taking a shot at the Perris Police Department for not raiding the known gang members house.

"It look's like they're circling a young black kid, how many of them are there?" Samuel said this while looking at Trump Cards already done math.

"It say's 20 so it look's like we got a 19 on 1. It's probably just a young kid from the neighborhood trying to get to school. These stupid gang's don't leave anybody alone." Samuel said feeling bad for the young kid.

"You see that gray car parked in the middle of the street?" Brian asked.

"Yeah what in the hell do we got going on this morning?" Samuel could clearly see the outlines of the weapons that sat on the laps of the two people inside of the gray car.

"There it go's! Look's like they're going to stab the kid." Brian narrated to Samuel. "He's down. Look the gray car's moving slow. That's Macho by the door. There has to be about 12 gun's in that house."

They watched a black man climb onto the moving car and fire a shotgun blast at the crowd. They all scattered and some fell.

"This is really nut's." Samuel said as they watched the driverless car roll down the street with the man on it. The would-be driver ran firing at the house falling face first as if he had been shot. Macho standing on his porch firing a high powered weapon at the car topped the image off for the two agents.

"It was like the old west out there this morning." Samuel said with a chuckle.

Brian wasn't smiling. He was still looking at the screen following the kid who was the center of everybodies attaintion this morning.

"Look he's with a girl now. They ran into a middle school." Brian said looking at Samuel as if pleading to get out there and help the kid.

"Alright that's enough of that stuff, let me get on it, I have to check on some things." Samuel said.

"What kind of things are you talking about?" Brian looked at Samuel with a grin as he rolled his chair away from the controls of Trump Card.

"Personal stuff." Samuel grined back.

*

Being a private dentist had all kind of perks for Lisa. She not only made the big bucks but she also had short work day's. With only four patients at most for a day she regularly was done with her day's work by 11:30a.m..

Samuel pinpointed his wife inside of her dental office with the infrared camera. Lisa's heat signatures gave off signs of a petite feminine creature. Samuel watched the two patients she had scheduled for the day. They were both taken care of by 10a.m., an easy day for Lisa.

Samuel held the power to monitor every cell phone plus home phone in the United States. Trump Card sent a signal to a phones receiver activating it. Listening devices were a thing of the past for the CIA. Today every American carried one with them wherever they went. Their cell phones!

Samuel had made a promise to himself that he would never use the power of the CIA to spy on his wife. He actually had held that promise. Well until...

Until his wife started treating him diferently. Instead of, "Oh baby you home, good! I got something extra special for you tonight." The strip tease before climbing into bed shown as bright as day in his mind.

Now arriving home late brought more of a, "The kid's are asleep, dinners in the fridge. And oh yeah! Can you sleep in the living room? I don't need you waking me when you come in."

Sleep in the living room? Are you freaking kidding me? His wife had yearned to make love to him every night. She claimed she needed to be sexed up by her husband nightly. Why then the month of, "Don't touch me Sam!"? Was somebody piping her down before he could get to her? He was ready to find out.

Lisa had refused to talk to him about their sexless nights. What else was he supposed to do?

"Hey girl what's up?" Lisa smiling into her office phones receiver.

"You Know! The same hot bodies here." Rita worked at a 24-hour fitness.

"I'm off in 30-minutes you want to grab something to eat?" Rita asked.

"Oh great! I'm done for the day. So where would you like to meet?"

"I'll see you at the Promenade's food court by the robot rock band." The Promenade was the name of Temecula's shopping mall.

"Awesome! See you there Rita!"

Samuel's wife had never told him about a friend named Rita. The girl sounded young. She must be trouble. Samuel did a quick search of the girl's history. The 24-hour fitness had her listed as 20 year old Rita Morales of Temecula. What was

his 32 year old wife doing having lunch with a 20 year old kid?
Were they hunting men? Maybe...

Samuel needed to know.

*

Brian left the Red Room to let his friend take care of
his personal things. Whatever that was he didn't care.

"Hey what's up Benson you still here?" Pollard stated
while Johnson sat next to him at the controls of a Predator Drone.
Johnson flew the Drone high above Cabazon checking out female
shoppers. Johnson was playing a game with Pollard. Who could
get the most nipple shots from unsuspecting women who merely
bent forward an inch to far. Pollard had two and Johnson was
stalking his third when Benson walked up. Johnson quickly switched
to viewing wind farms. The wind turbine spun on the screen.

"Yeah I'm always here Pollard, and stop fucking around
with the Drones! You know the feed go's back to the Pentagon
from your test flights." Pollard's face brightened red when he
thought about higher up's seeing his peeping and his name logged
in as the Pilot.

"Yes sir we're good. Just watching the wind." Pollard
responded.

Brian entered the elevator that led to a stairwell where
he could exit the bunker. Brian was going to his apartment to
get some sleep before his next shift in 6 hours.

When Brian left the room Pollard said, "Do you really
think the feed go's to the Pentagon?"

"No way man. We're the CIA. Nobody review's our shit."

"I sure hope so. Anyway's log in under your name if you want to keep messing around. It's my test flight."

"Well here you go Pollard." Johnson rolled away from the controls. "Fly it to the moon."


\*


Samuel watched his wife's every move. Lisa left her office and drove across a busy street to the Promenade's parking lot. She found a spot to park near the entrance to the food court. "How lucky!" She thought.

"How lucky!" He thought. Their minds were similar.

Rita worked next to the mall and also lived with her sister a block away. She walked to meet Lisa in the mall's food court. By the robot rock band as agreed.

Samuel could nolonger see them under the roof of the mall but he could follow their body heat. The two heat signatures came together as if embracing. A hug. They must be good friends. Samuel knew about all of her good friends. Why not this one? He activated the receiver to his wife's cell phone.

"Damn girl you looking good in them yoga pants!" Lisa said. Rita's heat signature grew brighter.

"I know I do huh. You look extra sexy yourself! What you wearing a thong under those scrubs?" Rita said leaning back to look at Lisa's butt playfully.

"Naw girl you know I ain't wearing no thong! I don't wear

any panties on day's I get to spend with you."

Rita smiled when Lisa said this. The 20 year old Rita knew she had the older Lisa hooked on her young ass. Plus the lady was married. To a man! Some important man at that. Lisa wouldn't say what kind of job, only that he spent many hours away from home and that she was happier for it.

Samuel sat steaming behind the controls of Trump Card as he listened to the flirtatious talk between his wife and this young hussy. His no good perfect smile perfect body perfect face having ass wife was cheating on him! With a woman. A young woman! Damn that bitch! Samuel wanted to take a Predator Drone, fly to the mall, and chop her ass down!

But Samuel couldn't do such a thing. He was just fuming in his mind. Samuel continued to watch but shut off his wife's cell phone receiver. He had to gather himself so he could calmly call his wife and tell her he wasn't coming home that night. Samuel was heartbroken.

Lisa drove Rita home. Instead of Lisa departing she entered the house too.

The bodies collided as soon as the front door shut behind them. Their heat signatures grew bright red as they found a place to lie. The sexual romp went on for an hour.

Samuel began to grind his teeth.

## Chapter-4

    Champ and Sofia arrived to their middle school's **nurse's** office. The school nurse quickly rose out of her chair to approach the bleeding boy. "Oh my! What happened to you?" The nurse led Champ to a chair. "Take a seat you will be okay."

    "Some guy's beat him up!" Sofia said angerly.

    "Sofia I'm okay. Go to class." Champ wished to get cleaned up and go to class himself. He was scheduled to take a History test he knew he was going to Ace. Champ was excited for it. Another A. Possible plus! Champ was in love with learning.

    "Yes Sofia I'll be taking care of your friend, now get to class." The school nurse ordered.

    "Alright." Sofia said looking sad, anxious. "Bye! I'll see you at lunch Champ." Sofia walked off to get to class.

    Champ watched her exit the nurse's office. He loved Sofia.

    "So tell me what happened? Did somebody beat you up?"

The school nurse removed the bottem of Champs shirt from around his forearm.

"No, I just fell on my walk to school. Hurt my arm pretty bad." The nurse had already cleaned the blood from Champs nose. Luckily it no longer bled.

"Come on now! Do I look stupid to you?" Everybody seemed to think he thought they were stupid today.

"No you don't ma'am, you look really smart."

"The school nurse let out a sigh, "Is your mother home, or do you have a nuber where we can contact your parents at work?"

"No. My mother works in L.A. and my fathers in prison."

"Well we need somebody to come and get you. The cut on your arm is pretty deep. You are going to need stitches."

"Really, It's that bad? I wanted to go to class today. I have to take a test, I can't miss it!"

"Sorry kiddo that's not going to happen." She covered Champs wound with butterfly bandages then slowly wrapped it with gauze. "You sure that you don't want to tell me who did this to you?"

"I would if somebody had done something to me but I don't know how it happened! I like fell on some glass and hit my face, it happened in the alley on the way here."

"Okay well just stay right there I need to go talk to someone. I will be right back." The nurse exited her office.

Champ would refuse to place himself where a shooting had just occurred. His mother had alway's told him, "If you ever

see a crime tell the police you didn't see anything. If you tell
them you saw something the person who did the crime will come
to hurt us!"

This thought was hardwired into Champs brain. He waited
for a few minutes then got up to leave the nurses office. As
Champ stepped through the door a voice summoned him, "Um Champ
where are you going? I need you to come over here."

The school nurse waved Champ over to the school's police
officers office. The school had two officers assigned to it from
the Perris Police Department. Champ walked slowly over to officer
Guzman's office. Officer Guzman stood next to the school nurse
with an unwelcoming look about him.

"Champ this officer will be taking you to the hospital
since your parents are not available."

"Hey Champ! That's a nice name, Champ. It's a winner's
name. Anyway I'm officer Guzman." The police officer stopped
speaking, stuck his hand out and waited for a responce.

Champ shook the officers hand but didn't say a word, just
looked passed him.

"Well uh I'll just run you over to the hospital to get
that arm stiched up. Then I'll be taking you stright home. Is
that okay with you Champ?"

"Yeah that's fine with me but can you bring me back to
school after the hospital? I really want to get to my history
class." Champ looked beggingly at the officer.

Officer Guzman looked over at the school nurse as if searching
for permission to bring the kid back to school. The nurse looking
back at the officer poked her bottom lip out shaking her head
up and down in approval.

"I don't see why not Champ," The officer smiled brightly at him, "Now let's hurry up and get out of here so we can get you back."

Champ followed officer Guzman to his patrol car, "Mind riding in the back Champ? I have some papers in the front and you don't want your friends from 6th Street seeing you in the passenger seat of a cop car."

Champ didn't respond but did hop in the back seat of the patrol car. Why did the officer mention 6th Street? He didn't have friends from there. The only friends Champ had were his mother, Sofia, and his school teachers. Champ sat back on the hard surface of the backseat. He felt like he was missing something? His backpack! Champs history test were in there. And where did he leave it? He got sick when he realized that he left it on 7th Street. Right where the shooting took place! 'No way did I do that?' He thought to himself, 'I'm just going to deny it. Somebody stole my backpack, that's it! That's what I will tell them!'

The patrol car slowed down as it drove by 7th street. The police officer Guzman looked at Champ in his rearview mirror. Champs head was glued to the right. The police were midway down the street with yellow caution tape up. Champ spotted his backpack lying in the street just a few feet inside of the yellow tape.

"What's going on down there Champ?" The officer's gaze went from the road back to looking at Champ through his mirror.

Champ visibly swallowed his saliva. "I don't know, it was hard to see."

"Probably some of your friends right? You guy's hate the P-13's. Some kind of turf war going on?"

"Oh I don't know, I don't have any friends." Saying this

sadly Champ put his face in his hands. 'Why did I leave my backpack?' He thought to himself.

Officer Guzman sensing Champs sadness said, "What's wrong buddy? Do you want to talk to me about something?"

"No, I'm just really sick. Can we please get to the hospital?" Champ leaned to his left and puked his mothers omelets on the backseat.

"Hang on buddy I'm getting you there." The officer sped up his vehicle.

*

Champ knew the officer wasn't his buddy. They walked into the emergency room at the small Perris Valley Hospital. Officer Guzman signed the boy in and escorted him through double swinging door's. In a hospital bed to their left Champ saw the Devil staring at him, pointing with a barely lifted finger.

"Hey Champ there go's your friend right there! Bone. Isn't that his name?" Officer Guzman had his right hand on Champs shoulder forcing the boy to face Bone.

Two plain clothes detectives where at the bedside. "So that's the kid that did all of this shooting, that little guy right there, while you and your brother just happened to be driving to the liquor store?" The Shirm had kept Bone from dying right away from his blood loss. Shirm had a way of making people super human. At least until their high went away then they went brain dead, or dead dead. The doctors considered it a miracle that Bone was still conscious. It wouldn't last long and the detectives knew they had to take advantage of this if they hoped to solve the shooting case on 7th Street.

In a whisper Bone made his final statement to the detectives. "That lil niggas from the turf. He shoot all them people. Me and my brother didn't do anything." Bone flat lined. Life is funny. Bone spent his 32-years hating the police but his last few seconds of life was spent with them. Score 1 for the police. The game was over for Bone.

"I don't know him! I don't know what the hell this is! I want my mom! Call my mom!" Champ cried and pulled away from officer Guzman. The two detectives as if instinctively rushed forward to grab Champ. He bolted towards the door's and reached them before any officer could grab him. The chase was on.

Champ ran because he needed air. He couldn't breath with the police around him. 'Why were they framing me? I didn't do anything. I should have just told them what happened. Then they would have made me a witness. I would be gun down in the street. In my house. My mother would be hurt. I have to get away from these dumb ass police!' Champ ran across the street from the hospital to a row of houses. As he slid over the wooden fence into a backyard the gauze on his left arm scrapped the top of the fence. The wound started to bled again, the pain came back.

"Stop you little piece of shit!" The heavy detective broke down the fence as he attempted to go over it. Falling on his hands he was back up and after Champ.

As Champ was getting ready to leap for another fence the 6-foot 230 pound detective came like a bowling ball crashing into the 5'8 130-pound Champ.

"AWWW!" Champ screamed out in pain as the detective drove Champs face into the wooden fance, then dead grass.

"You stupid gangbanger sonofabitch! Don't you ever run from me! You got that?" The detective lifted Champ to his feet, escorting him out of the backyard holding Champs hands behind

his back by his fingers. Champs nose bled again. He was in too
much pain to speak, Champ quietly wept.

The detectives partner and officer Guzman joined them
on the sidewalk across from the hospital.

"Damn Clark! He is only a kid! What in the hell did you
do to him?" Officer Guzman questioned the detective.

This pissed the detective off. "This kid is a fucking
murderer who shot three people this morning! He's lucky I didn't
blow his fucking head off! And who are you to question me? Go
back to your stupid middle school job and leave the murderers
to us okay!" The detective squeezed on Champs fingers tightly,
as he stared down officer Guzman.

"You're way out of line with your comments. I will be
going to my Captain with this. Until then I am not going to leave
the kid in your custody." Officer Guzman stated while matching
the detectives stare.

"You want him? Take the fucking animal!" The detective
letting go of Champs fingers, recklessly shoved him over to officer
Guzman who put a firm grip on Champs upper left arm.

"Just make sure you get him back to the station. He's
our number one murder suspect." The detectives marched off to
their unmarked patrol car while Officer Guzman walked Champ back
to the hospital.

Champ was grateful Officer Guzman stood up to the detective
for him. Champ thought the detective was going to kill him. After
Champs forearm was stitched up he was taken to the Perris Police
Department. On the drive there Officer Guzman spoke with him.
"You know Champ you really need to tell us your side of what
happened today. Those guy's at the station are going to question
you until you give us a straight answer. I think you're a good

guy, I just want to hear your side of the story."

"I know. If I tell you what happened can you take me home?"

"Yeah, I'm sure we can arrange for something like that once we get to the station."

"Okay this is what happened. I was walking to school up 7th Street like I do every morning. Before I get to A Street some Mexicans started harassing me, calling me nigger and names in Spanish. I tried to ignore them and keep walking but a bunch of them surrounded me. One of them pulled out a knife and I hit it away with my arm. I got cut, then he socked me. I fell on my back a little dazed. Next thing I know that guy who was in the hospital bed. It was him. He started shooting people! As soon as he went by me I got up. I forgot my backpack. I ran to school for the nurse. I told her I fell because I was scared, you know? To be around a shooting. I didn't want to tell!"

"No, it's good Champ. You're not telling. But what about that girl the nurse told me you came in with?"

"What girl?" Champ wan not going to bring Sofia into this.

Officer Guzman parked in the back secured area of the Police Department.

"Now just tell the detectives everything you stated to me. I'm sure they'll let you go home." Officer Guzman knew Champ wasn't going home. He looked even more guilty at this point than the last kid did. That kid was now sitting in Juvenile Hall facing murder charges.

"Damn it Clark you gave that kid too much information when you went on your rant. You have to let him spit out the information that only somebody who was guilty would know." Detective Williams was detective Clark's partner of 6 years. They worked for the Riverside County Sheriff Central Homicide Division.

"I know it, I just let my anger get the best of me."

Officer Guzman interupted the two detectives, "I got your
kid on the holding bench. Here is the tape of a statement he
gave me on the way from the hospital. It might help you guy's.
Good luck!"

Both detectives thanked the Officer for his assistance
as he left. Champ was escorted into an interrogation room, told
to sit in the chair facing the door, he did. The room was small
with what looked like carpet on all four wall's. Champ was scared,
stressed, tired. Thinking of his mother wishing she could save
him. Linda would arrive home from work in four hours. Champ wished
he would be there to greet her. What a big hug she would be in
for.

Champ was questioned on and off for eight hours. Tired
and groggy he wanted his mother. Champ told the detectives his
**version** of what took place.

"That's bullshit!" They scloded him. "Your big homey Lazy's
in the next room telling us this is your idea. You wanted to
rob Macho's house. You talked Lazy and Bone into going with you,
it would be an easy target. Things get hairy during the robbery,
so Macho's friends show up. You take a sawed-off shotgun from
your backpack. Blast some guy's. Macho fearing for his safety
put's a bullet in your friend. He dies. Luckily the three people
you shot survived. We found your backpack and shotgun at the
scene. Who's fingerprints do you think we found on the gun? Your
story about walking to school, that's crap! We have over a dozen
witnesses plus your own homeboy's ratting you out. You are running
out of options Champ! Just tell us why you went to Macho's house.
If Bone and Lazy say,'come with us Champ, we need you to stand
right here while we rob this house.'. That's okay Champ. You
go home for that. We just need you to say, Okay I understand

this was wrong, I didn't mean any harm. I was just a lookout for those guy's, they start shooting, you didn't want no part of this. You run to school and fall on the way. That explains your cut. You're good Champ! You get to go home! But not if you continue this I didn't know anything bullshit! You're looking at life Champ. One murder and three attempted. You're done!"

Champ refused to cry but he wanted to. If he told them what they wanted to hear they insisted he would be going home. He was going to do it.

"That's it man, the lookout thing. They say stand right here. I listen to him." Champ admitted he was a lookout to the robbery and repeated the detectives lookout theory. Champ sealed his own fate with the statement.

Champ was booked into Riverside Juvenile Hall for 1st degree murder and three counts of attempted murder.

*

When Linda arrived home from work she nearly fainted when calling for Champ with no response. Linda hurriedly went through every room. Then outside. She went from street to the alley calling out Champs name. Where in the hell was her boy?

"Linda is everything alright?" Carrol peeking her head out from apartment-1. A thin nightgown covered the woman.

"Have you seen Champ anywhere? I can't find him!" Champ was alway's home when his mother arrived.

"No. I was out earlyer and I never saw him come home from school. You should call the school."

"Good idea!" Linda went to get her cell phone from the house. Nobody answered, the school was closed. Linda grabbed her car key's. She drove slowly up 6th Street looking for her son. Linda called 911 and told them that her 14 year old son was missing. They explained to her a person had to be gone for a period of 24 hours before they could report them as missing. They took Champs name telling Linda that they would call if they found him.

Not even five minutes pass when Linda receives a call from detective Clark. He told Linda they had her son. That he was hanging out with bad people. They were currently interrogating him. Linda demanded she be allowed to see her son. In response she was told she would be contacted after the interrogation. Linda was so angry at how the police were treating her that she drove to the police station. An Officer working at the front desk informed her she had to wait outside. A detective would come out to speak with her.

Linda awoke in her car at three in the morning. She was still in the Police Departments parking lot. Storming into the Police Station there was a different Officer working the front desk. Linda asked for her son.

"He was moved to Riverside Juvenile Hall and booked in for murder." The sleepy officer informed Linda.

Linda's ear's burned when the sound of murder left the Officers mouth. Linda left in tears. This was not happening.

*

Champ and Linda both could not sleep from their respective bed's. They thought of each other. Stressed, worried, cried.

Champ was shackled in leg and waist chains. Two group counselors escorted the accused killer. Stripped of personal clothes Champ wore white velcro shoes, kaki pants and yellow shirt. The shirt's color represented the highest sercurity level. The weight of the blankets and sheets Champ carried made his cuff's seem tighter. He would bare the cuff marks for a day or two. When Champ got to Group-9 (High Security) he was ordered to drop everything in his hands to the dirty floor. Kneeling on a bench the counselors removed the shackles. When removed blood was visible through Champs socks. Tight shackles cut deep! The counselors did this rutine nightly. They'd seen worse. Champ picked up his bedding. Escorted to cell-12 the door shut. Locked. It was dark. The outside cell window was tinted. Moonlight struggled to shine through. The lights would not be turned on for him. Champ was scared. What had just happened?

Champ threw a sheet over the mattress, crawled under a blanket. Getting into the fetal position he cried!

## Chapter-5


Brian and agent kim Bryant arrived to the bunker at the same time. 5:40p.m.. Kim went to relieve Pollard and Johnson, while Brian went to relieve his good buddy Samuel from the Red Room. Brian typed the first pass code in. Access denied!

Only Samuel Richerdson had high enough security clearance for a program called "Ghost". Brian knew the name of the program. That was all. He marvelled at the possibilities.

While Ghost was accessed only Samuel could be in the Red Room. If one managed to enter, the Red Room would simply shut down the program in a flash. The same controls used for Trump Card were used for Ghost.

Brian's access to the Red Room was not granted until 6:05p.m.. 'What the hell was Samuel up to?' he thought to himself.

"Man trying to keep me from work Sam?"

"No, not at all! Just had to get some work done for the guy's in D.C."

"Any word on when I might get clearance for Ghost?"

"Matter of fact we did speak on the matter."

"What did they say?"

"They're full at the moment but your about 8th on their list."

Getting clearance for Ghost required a two week trip to D,C. for training. Then you may be assigned to a new base where needed  Rumor had it that not even the president knew about Ghost. Brian wanted to be a part of that club.

"I'll see you in the morning Brian, I have a dinner date with Lisa."

"Have fun boss. Oh yeah and get me a paper when you come in tomorrow will you?"

"What the hell do you want a paper for?"

"Few stories I wanted to check on."

"U.S.A. Today, L.A. Times or The Press Enterprise?"

"I need The Press Enterprise."

"Alright I'll see you tomorrow Brian." Samuel left the Red Room.

"Good evening Mr. Richerdson."

"You have a good evening as well Kim." Samuel smiled at

the young lady as he got in the elevator to leave.

*

"What's up with Ron?" Brian asked. He left the Red Room and took a seat next to Kim.

"Look's like they got him assigned to holding off the Ethiopian's near the border." The satellite held Ron's location on the screen in a small town near the border with Etheopia.

Ron called base from a house where he held sniper duty for the clan.

"Ron this is Benson and Bryant go ahead?" Brian said.

"Good to hear you guys. I'm assigned to snipe incoming Ethiopian troop's that are on foot. There is an ambush set up for them around my position.

"Ron we have the Ethiopian's on screen with tanks, helicopters, and heavy artillery. Your clan will be overpowered." Kim said.

"That's really motivating!" Ron lied. It had took his hope of surviving for the day away. He knew what to expect when he accepted the CIA mission to infiltrate the clan.

"Who's in charge?" Brian asked.

"Some young 23 year old kid got the job. He is in a heavy machine gun position a block to the east."

"Ron tell him you saw the Ethiopian's tanks and that your guy's will be wiped out if you don't fall back to another city with a stronger opposition." Brian said

"Brian this kid is a suicidal killer. That's why the higher up's chose him for this. He will never retreat. If I leave my position I'm exposed. If my own clan doesn't shoot me the Ethiopian's will!"

"Alright just be invisible Ron, we need you!" Brian said.

"We'll gather intel at a later date. Be safe Ron." Kim said.

The conversation was over but Ron would be monitored by a satellite. Ron could not wear an earpiece because no clan member wore them. They all had cell phones and this was Ron's only method of talking to the CIA Base.

Brian left Kim for the Red Room where he would be granted permission to use the Trump Card that was over Somalia. He had an agent in the field in a live war. Trump Card gave Brian a front row seat.

*

When Samuel called his wife he told her what he witnessed. Not explaining how. Only that he knew about Rita and her sexual encounters with the woman. Lisa was angry that her husband had used the power of the CIA to spy on her. Something he promised never to do.

The girl's were in the living room watching T.V. before dinner. It was 5:59p.m.. Lisa took her screaming to the back yard. Two feet away from her sliding glass door in the back yard Lisa stopped yelling.

The bullet that entered the top of her skull nearly ripped her body in half. The thud of her body hitting the ground could

be heard from inside of the house. The oldest  Jasmine was the
first to see her mothers body. She would have nightmares for
life.


*


   Samuel hung up his phone when his wife stopped yelling
at him. He had to get home in time for dinner.

   Brian answered his phone. "Samuel what's up?"

   "Brian my...my wife. She's been shot!"

   "What! What happened?"

   "I don't know? There was officers around my house when
I arrived home, they found her in our backyard. Somebody murdered
her." Samuel's voice was calm.

   "Your daughters?"

   "They're safe, but  Jasmine saw the shooting. I'm taking
them to their grandparents in Hemet tonight. I have to get on
this Brian. Find out if my wife was the target or  is somebody
trying to send me a message?"

   "I'm online now, I'll go over there! I was covering Somalia
that may have been the reason I  missed it."

   "Look for a high caliber weapon in the area and pull up
the feed from earlier."

   "Okay I'm there. This is strange Samuel! Lisa drops at
6p.m. but there was no gunshot."

"There had to be a gunshot; Brian, my wife was shot in the head!"

"I'm not disputing that but maybe there was a malfunction that kept it from being picked up?"

"That's never happened before."

"I know."

"Come to now and check the area Brian."

"Alright I got something! We have a rifle in the house directly behind your's. In an upstairs bedroom, window faces your backyard."

"Brian I need you to call in an anonymous tip that you saw the shot come from that bedroom window."

"I'll do that right now. How are you holding up Sam?"

"I'll be okay. I'm going to give a statement, drop the girl's off in Hemet, then I'm coming into the office."

"Okay, be safe!"

The conversation ended. Samuel gave a statement to the lead detective assigned to the case. Samuel told the officer about the 22 year old white man that still lived with his parents in the home behind his. A night prior he opened his window threatening samual and his wife while they drunk wine, listening to music quietly in their backyard. According to Samuel the man told the couple he would shoot them if they didn't turn off their fag music.

With Samuel's statement plus the anonymous tip, the police would search the home, more important the man's bedroom. Finding the rifle, possible murder weapon, he would be charged with the senseless murder of a mother of two. A white man assassinating a black woman while her daughters watched. He didn't stand a chance in court. Samuel could care less about the innocence of the man. He was a 22 year old punk rocker who freeloaded off of his rich parents. Life in prison would teach him to grow up.

Samuel  retrived his daughters from the police station. After leaving his daughters with their grandma and grandpa, he would return to the base at March.

*

The door to cell 12 opened. Champ ripped the blanket from over his head. He needed to tell whomever had opened the door that he needed to go home. It was Saturday morning. Champs mother would take him to the beach in Oceanside. He would boogy board then walk to McDonalds under the pier where he could get chicken strips and a milk shake.

Opening his eye's there was a Hispanic kid wearing a yellow shirt with kaki pants. The kid placed a breakfast tray on Champs cell sink without looking at him then left his cell. Before the group counselor could shut the cell door Champ sat up, "Wait I'm supposed to go home!"

Almost shut the counselor reopened the door fully. "Didn't you just get here last night?"

"Yeah I did but I'm not supposed to be here. I need to talk to my mom!"

"They didn't give you a call yesterday?"

"No they didn't, it was too late."

"Alright I'll check on it."

"Please do, I'm supposed to go home..." The door shut as Champ was still pleading. Champ was all alone. Just him and his breakfast. Champ looked at the pancakes and oatmeal. He was too sick to eat. He had never been confined to such a room before. Champ drank his milk and stood at the thin cell window on the cell door.

There were two kid's going in and out of cell's delivering breakfast tray's. Champ could see cell 1 to cell 10 to his right and cell's 18-20 to his left. One counselor opened and closed door's while another wrote stuff down at a staff table. Champ wanted to but didn't cry for fear of another inmate seeing him.

When they finished passing out tray's the two Hispanic inmates sat down to eat. The staff member went into the staff office sat down and started a phone conversation. Champ knew he was forgotten. He remebered being booked into juvenile hall for murder robbery but he didn't believe it. Champ lied down, he hated this hopeless feeling.

It was now time for the tray's to be picked up. Champ sat up again. The staff told him to hold on and he would come back and speak with him. Champ paced in his small cell until the staff member came back. 30-minutes later.

"Your name is Washington?"

"Yes sir!" Champ replied.

"I'm Mr. Weldon, over at the table is Mr. Lynch. This is our unit, Group-9. What did you come in for?"

"They said something about a burglary but I didn't do anything." Champ said not wanting to accept the word murder.

"What happened to your arm?"

"Somebody cut me with a knife, that's why they're blaming me for robbing somebody."

"Does it hurt?"

"Yeah, a little bit."

"I'll have the nurse check you out when she comes up here. In the mean time you have to stay in your room until tomorrow. When you come out you bring your hygiene bag and set it by your door. Tuck in your shirt, put on your shoes, then you have a seat in a line. No talking sit up straight with your arm's around you knees. We workout, play some sports, then go to school. Do you have any questions?"

"Can I please call my mother? She doesn't even know where I am at."

"I'll see what I can do, there's no promises."

Champ went back to his bed and covered his head. Not crying anymore just blocking the cell light and wanting to disappear.

Champ awoke to lunch being served in the same manner as breakfast. For lunch was a burnt square piece of pizza with ravioli. A small salad sat in one slot of the tray. Champ was so hungry he ate the salad by hand, swallowed the ravioli in three bites, then covering his pizza with a ranch dressing packet he took his time to savor the flavor. Gulping down his half pint of milk Champ felt like he could take on ten of those lunches.

At 1p.m. the cell door opened. Champ snapped out of his sleep jumping to his feet, "What is it? What? Am I going home?"

"Calm down!" Mr. Weldon yelled while pulling his pepper

spray out, holding it at the ready.

Champ stood silently anxiously waiting to hear why Mr. Weldon was opening his cell door.

"You have a visit but if you can't handle it I'll cancel it!"

No I can handle it! Please let me have my visit?" Champ was ready to tear up.

"Okay. Your mothers over there." Mr. Weldon pointed Champ in the direction of Linda who sat accross from an empty chair. Her face lit up when she saw her baby. Linda wanted to cry but she had to be strong for her son.

"Oh baby I'm so sorry." Linda's eye's watered as she held Champ tight.

Champ cried, "Mom they won't let me leave but I didn't do anything."

"It's okay Champ, we'll get through this."

"I know but I didn't do anything and I'm in juvenile hall. Did they tell you why they won't let me go home?"

"I asked when I called here. They told me you have court monday. They charged you with murder Champ. What did you do, what happened to your arm?"

"Mom it was the Mexicans on 7th Street. They jumped me on my way to school and cut me with a knife. I got up and ran to school when Lazy and Bone from up the street started shooting people."

"I can't believe nobody told me about you getting stabbed.

I'm going to get you out of here, it's just going to take some
time. What were you doing with those older guy's Champ?"

"I wasn't with them mom! They came by after I got stabbed.
Bone died. I saw him in the hospital. He told the police I shot
those people."

"Oh dear I'm so sorry your going through this. I will
talk to your father, he'll know what to do. He was in the same
situation when he was your age. Just remeber to stay strong.
All of this wrong will only strengthen your soul. God will take
care of you. You're my baby. He has too!" Linda smiled at Champ
with her last sentence.

This smile with the words warmed Champ. "Do you think
I will go home Monday?"

"Hopefully!" Linda said really not sure.

*

Champ was transferred early Monday morning for court.
To save money Riverside County moved away from local courts and
now relied on regional courthouses. The Southwest Courthouse
in Murrieta, Downtown Riverside, Banning, and Indio. In 2001
Champ would have been taken to the courthouse off of D Street
in downtown Perris. Being that it was 2003 the van Champ was
being transferred in passed the D Street off-ramp as the 215-
freeway narrowed from three to two lanes and snaked it's way
through downtown Perris.

The looming castle faded away as the van moved closer
to Murrieta. Being that the crime Champ was charged with committing
occurred south of Ryder Street Champ had to face the tuff Judges
of the Southwest Courthouse.

Southwest juvenile hall was only a year old. Much newer than the over 100 year old juvenile hall in Riverside. At Southwest Champ was given blue pants and shorts with S.W.J.H. printed on them. Same yellow security shirt as Riverside.

Champ was driven to a back area of the four story courthouse. Four holding tanks for the juvenile hall kid's. Champ was put in a large holding tank with four kid's also wearing yellow shirts.

"What's up homey, where you from?" A inshape looking 16 year old black kid asked Champ. A fat white kid and two also fit Mexicans looked at the black kid's confrontation.

"I ain't from nowhere." Champ responded glad everybody wore waist chains. The thought was that this would keep him from getting pounded by the hulking kid.

"I'm Raw Dog from 4-Corner Hustler Crip. Where they got you at?"

"I'm Champ, they got me in Riverside but I came here for court."

"They will probably put you in Group-2 with us. The fat White boy is Jason." Raw Dog pointed.

"What's up Champ!" Jason said.

The two Mexican kid's stood whispering in a corner of the holding tank as Raw Dog introduced them to Champ. "That's Rascal on the left from Hemet and Frank from San Jacinto on the right."

"What's up dog!" Frank said.

"Where do you live?" Rascal asked.

"I stay off of 6th Street in Perris." Champ answered.

"Perris! Damn it's about nine of you mothafuckas in Group-2." Raw Dog said adding, "There's an open cell, cell 21 on the bottom tier you'll probably go to. The unit is cool. We workout a lot. On Friday's we have our football tournaments. The winning team get's pizza or hot wings on Saturday. Everybody get's along but every now and then we have a fight."

"How many people are in the unit?" Champ asked.

"There's twenty cell's. Cell 20-29 on the bottom and 30-39 on the top tier. Cell 20 is Rascal, cell 22 is Chubby from Perris." When Champ heard Chubby's name he had a flashback to 7th Street. Could this possibly be the same Chubby that stabbed him? Champs face didn't reveal his frightening thoughts and Raw Dog continued with his rundown of Group-2. "Cell 23 is a Mexican named silent from Temecula, next to him is Flaco from Perris, then Daffy from Perris, a brotha named Dino from Perris Locs, Fat Boy Jason from everywhere, Blacky a Mexican from Lake Elsinore, and Dino's homeboy Y.G. from Perris Locs. The top tier is me in cell 30, then Duce from Neighborhood Perris, a Mexican named Spider from Perris, a brotha Shorty from Rubidoux P.J.'s, Frank is in cell 34, Shadow from Corona, Midget from L.A., Adam from Riverside, Frog from Perris, and the homey Smash G from Moreno Valley. For staff we have Mr. Abukutsa or Mr. A, Mr. Henderson in the morning, and Ms. Pixley and Mr. Gomez at night. Ms. Miller works mornings or nights."

"Man! How do you know everybody?" Champ asked amazed at how much Raw Dog seemed to know about Group-2.

"I've been down two years little homey! I was the first kid to ever be housed in Group-2."

Raw Dog, Jason, Frank, and Rascal were all led out of the holding tank at the same time. They told Champ they were in adult court.

Everybody in the juvenile hall's security unit was in
adult court. The group went in the elevator, Champ was left behind
in the holding tank. The staff told Champ he was going to juvenile
court. He took it as a good sign.

Thirty minutes later Champ was going up an elevator. On
the 4th Floor Champ was escorted out of the elevator and into
another holding tank. In the holding tank was a skinny white
man with wire rimmed glasses. His gray suit could have more properly
fit a man twice his size.

"Hello Champ! How are you doing? I am your lawyer, Mr.
Goodson!" The lawyer stuck his hand out smiling.

Champ reached as far as the chains allowed to shake Mr.
Goodson's hand.

"Can I go home today?" Champ asked. A staff member freed
Champs hand's so he could sign a form the lawyer handed him.

"You're not going home today. The D.A. is charging you
as an adult for 1st degree murder, three attempted murders, and
a buglary. The best I think I can do for you is try and get you
a half million dollar bail. Maybe some family members can get
together and get you out. These are some really serious charges
against you Champ. It's going to take me awhile to review everything
so today we will plead not guilty as a formality, then I will
see you again in two week's for your arraignment in adult court,
where we will plead not guilty again. I need you to sign that
paper that states you are pleading not guilty."

"Why do I have to plead not guilty twice?"

"Well because this hearing is for the D.A. to inform the
juvenile court that your case is being directly filed into adult

court."

"Will you be able to get me bail?"

"We will find out. I have some questions for you. In your statement to the police why did you tell them you went to rob Mr. Sanchez?"

"No. I only said that after I told them what happened to me. They didn't believe me. They said if I told them I was only a lookout I would go home. I didn't even do anything. I was a vitim but these stupid police made me say that I was a lookout. All I wanted was to go home, see my mom. The police knew that and used me!" Champ was breathing heavy, and talking louder. He wanted to punch the lawyer for saying he wasn't going home.

The lawyer took a few steps back as Champ balled his fist. "Now Champ calm down. Your in no position to get angry. That's why you are in this mess. Please just answer my questions, I'm here to help you."

"I am answering your, ugh... but nobody believes shit I say!" Mr. Goodson the lawyer was starting to look more like detective Clark to Champ who wanted to explode in a rage he had never felt before.

"I believe what you say Champ. Now how long have you known Lazy and his brother Bone?"

"I don't know them, they live up the street from me!"

"How long have you been a member of the... what is it... 6th Street," Pow!

Mr. Goodson dropped the file in his hands, his glasses flew off of the side of his face as his body was propelled into the wall behind him. The bone in his nose fractured when Champs knuckles made contact.

"Stop it!" Yelled the staff as he tackled Champ to the ground. The lawyer sat unconscious against the wall.

"What's going on back here?" The courts bailiff entered the holding tank engaging in restraining a fuming Champ.

"We need medical on 4th Floor holding!" The bailiff now stood and then bent next to the unconscious Mr. Goodson.

Champs hands were locked back into the waist chains only this time with his right hand in the left cuff and left hand in the right cuff. His arm's were crossed and locked in place so he could do no more damage to lawyer's noses. Mr. Goodson was transported to a hospital after regaining consciousness.

*

Champ stood infront of the juvenile court Judge. Arm's crossed, two bailiff's held his arm's in place.

The Judge spoke briefly. "Mr. Washington it disturbs me that our great nation could produce a 14 year old as violent as you. Unfortunately it is not up to me to pass judgment on you. That duty will rightfully be for an adult court Judge. What I will say is if I were the one sentencing you, not only because of the murders you're charged with, but for your blatant disrespect for me and this court by assaulting your attorney Mr. Goodson, I could only hope the law would allow me to incarcerate you for the rest of your life. As a matter of official duty I need to ask you, how do you plead?"

"I didn't do anything Mr. Judge, I swear! I want to go

home!"

"That's all for this court. The defendant pleads not guilty."
The Judge waved for the bailiff's to remove Champ from his courtroom.

Champ screamed while he was being forced from the courtroom.
"I didn't do anything! This is not fair!"

The door was shut on Champs voice so he could not be heard
in the now quite courtroom.

*

Linda took off from work to make her son's court appearance.
"Car trouble." she told her boss. The 4th Floor of the courthouse
was quite in the long hallway. She was told to wait and a bailiff
would come to get her when it was her son's turn to go infront
of the Judge. Other families (mainly sigle mothers) were called
before her. It was now 11:30p.m. and Linda entered the courtroom
to find out what was taking so long.

"Excuse me ma'am this courtroom is closed." A bailiff
said.

"It can't be. My son is supposed to be arraigned here
today."

"What is your son's name?" The bailiff checked the courts
docket.

"Champ Washington."

"Okay here it is Washington. He was arraigned at 9:15a.m.
this morning. Say's his case was transferred to the adult court
for arraignment in two weeks. Room 201."

"Two weeks! I was waiting in the hallway all morning to see my son, now you're telling me two weeks! I can't believe this!" Linda stormed from the courtroom before she said something her mother would never approve of. Linda went through this with Ky, now she was going through it with her son. She wanted to breakdown but remebered to herself, "Destiny is hard to beat!" She knew Champ was destined to do great things. God would see them through.

*

Champ was taken to Southwest juvenile hall. After being searched and booked into Southwest Champ was given a phone call. His mother did not answer her cell phone. Champ longed to hear his mothers voice after his ruff day at court.

Champ looked at the empty seats in the courtroom. Champ felt as if he were a hopeless slave to the mighty Roman Empire; in which he spent the last week studying for Friday's history test. A test he would never Ace due to the evil Mexicans on 7th Street. The evil white detective who tricked him into admitting guilt. The skinny lawyer who said, "Your not going home today!" The Judge who felt that he should die in prison.

Now Champ faced Group-2 where waiting in a dark cell next to his would be his tormentor. Champ was tired of flight. He was now ready to fight. Fight everyone and everything that kept him from his mother. Fight! Fight! Fight!

Chapter-6


Samuel dropped his girls off at their grandparents in
the city of Hemet. He was now driving west on the Romona Expressway.
The cow manure smell was strong as Samuel drove pass numerous
farms. The smell faded as he drove through the small town of
Nuevo. The Romona Expressway winded up a small hill as it enters
the Perris city limits. To Samuel's right was the Starwest dirt
bike track. Beyond the race track the rocky dam of Perris Lake
could be seen. The dam was structurally weak and the CIA had
it listed as one of the potential terrorist targets in Riverside
County. To Samuel's left were thousands of homes and a dozen
school's. A new eight lane freeway and thousands of more homes
were planned for the area. A strategically placed explosive device
would bury the entire Perris Valley in ten-feet of water. Luckily
the CIA would never allow any unauthorized explosives from reaching
the dam.

    " Richerdson." Samuel answered his cell phone. On the other
end a detective explained to Samuel that upon search of his neighbors
home a high power rifle was recovered in the room of the man

who was believed to have threatened them. Samuel thanked the detective and asked him to keep him posted if anything else were to come up.

Samuel arrived to March at 10p.m.. Kim was on the phone with her field agent Ron. Out of the 39 members of the clan only 14 survived the Ethiopian assault. The 23 year old kid in charge had his skull blown apart. Ron retreated to a safer position. Kim gathered all of the details.

Kim was surprised to see samual back at the base. Normally once leaving that was it. Samuel only came back at 6 in the morning for his next shift.

"Is everything okay sir?" Kim held Ron briefly away from her ear.

"Yes Ms. Bryant things are fine. I just have some business to tend to in the Red Room that's all." Samuel's face remained stern as he did the routine the Red Room required.

"Samuel, I'm really sorry brother." Brian poured a fresh brew into a cup for Samuel. Samuel needed the caffeine. It had been a long day for him, dealing with lot's of emotions he was normally good at controlling.

"Wow! Lisa is gone Brian. To a senseless act of violence. A terrorist act perpetrated by a young American kid."

"Why did he do it?"

"Who knows? We spend our lives saving others, now when something like this hit's home it makes me wonder, how do we stop violence when it is so random?"

"Do you want me to get Bill to take him off the locals hands, we can send him to Cuba?"

"No we will let the kid go to state. The California prison system will eat him alive. He will be treated better at Gitmo." Samuel Knew the fresh 22 year old would be turned into somebodies bitch on a level-4 prison yard. Resistance would only cost him his life.

"I'll give you some time alone Sam. I'm going to go assist Kim on the details with Ron." Brian walked toward the door to leave the Red Room.

"Brian I have to go to D.C. for a week. Assist Pollard and Johnson while I am gone, you have the drivers seat."

"Is it really that important? You need some time."

"I'm as well as I've ever been. We all die Brian. Even the people we love."

"Understood Sam but if you want to talk about it you have my number."

"I'll call you when I board a plane to return, until then don't forget to make sure nobody blows up the world."

"Alright." Brian closed the Red Room door and took a seat next to Kim.

"He kicked you out, you are not that important huh?" Kim gave Brian a playful look.

"Actually Miss Bryant I'm very important! I have been left in charge for the week." Brian smiled at Kim.

"What, you're going to be my boss?"

"For a little bit."

"What about our date at the drive-in Friday?"

"We'll see a movie next week. Not to change the subject but I think Ron did really well for himself for a live war."

"When do you think we can get another agent out there with him?"

"That could be a few years off. Ron has to gain enough rank so we can drop in a new guy smoothly. May even be an O.T.R.? No seasoned agent would take the job." An O.T.R. was an 'Off The Record' agent. One that can be any American citizen recruited for a specific CIA mission. An O.T.R. can become an official member of the CIA after completing a mission successfully.

Samuel exited the Red Room.

"Taking off already?" Brian asked Samuel.

"Yeah, got a plane waiting on the runway."

"That was fast!"

"It's the CIA, not Southwest Airlines!"

Brian chuckled at Samuel's responce.

Samuel boarded the military cargo plane that was going to Maryland. The plane ascended over Moreno Valley. Samuel sat back in his seat closing his eye's. His thoughts were not of his dead cheating wife or now motherless children. Samuel thought about his meeting with the president and head of the CIA. That is what got Samuel's blood pumping. His own importance in the world made his heart beat. His boss was the most powerful man on Earth. Samuel knew that would be him one day.

*

Raw Dog, Jason, Frank, Rascal, and Champ were led in a perfectly straight line by two staff members to Group-2. Southwest juvenile hall had four Units. A control booth was surrounded on all four sides by Groups-1,2,3, and 4. Group-1 had 19 cells while Group-2 had 20 cells for high security juveniles. Group-3 and 4 were identical with 10 cells on the bottom tier and 20 bunk beds on the top tier.

The kid's whispered about Champ on their slow walk to Group-2. Finally Raw Dog spoke up. "A Champ you really socked your lawyer man?"

"Yeah, I'm just tired of this shit. I'm in jail because somebody stabbed me, now I'm charged with murder, I can't believe it." Champ replied.

"That's messed up but we're all going through it. I'm facing 20 years for a buglary!"

"Damn, why 20 years?" Champ asked Raw Dog.

"I thought nobody was home but when I went in the front door a little white lady pulled a gun on me. She said if I ran she would shoot me. The lady reached for her phone and dropped the gun. I picked it up and ran off with it. Shit I didn't want her to shoot me! But 20 years is a long time. I've been fighting it for two years already."

Entering Group-2 the others took seats on floor mats infront of the T.V.. Mr. A escorted Champ to cell 21. Right there lying on a floor mat was Chubby.

Chubby smiled at Champ as he was escorted by.

"You have to be in your cell for 24 hours because you punched your lawyer. We will get you out tomorrow to program." Mr. A closed the cell door.

Champ stared at Chubby through the dark cell window. Chubby's smile faded as he could feel Champs cold stare eat his heart away. No knife, no gun, only four homey's to back him up. Sudden regret came over Chubby as he realized he would have to answer to one of his victim's tomorrow.

*

Tuesday morning Brian and Kim were having breakfast at a Denny's. Brian had a copy of the Press Enterprise.

'14-year old Champ Washington charged in a gang slaying of one and attempted slaying of three others, assualts his attorney before arraignment. Future arraignment set for adult court in two weeks.' That was the bold print to head off the story on the cover of the local section.

"You see this story right here? The local P.D. are so dumb. A simple check up on this kid and they would see that he is a straight A student, no gang ties really smart kid who spends most of his time with his girlfriend." Brian looked across the table at Kim who just slid a piece of cheesy omelet in her mouth.

"Yeah I see it Brian. If you don't mind me asking why so much interest in this case? Going soft on us?"

"No I'm not going soft, it's just after so many years of seening people get the short end of the stick, you know? It makes me feel bad for him."

Kim took the paper from Brian, "Let me see!"

She read a bit then looked at Champs mug shot plastered on the sections front page. "Hey the kid look's a little like Ron, we can send him to Somalia? Ha..Ha..!" Kim laughed at her own joke.

Brian just stared at Kim, not reacting to her joke. Just thinking.

"What? What is it?" Kim asked.

"You know that might just be a really great idea!"

"What idea?" Kim looked confused. Brian couldn't be talking about her joke.

"The one about the kid."

"There's no way! The kid's in jail charged with murdering people. How could we ever trust him?"

"It's been done before. Remember the Mexican Mafia guy I got out of Salinas Valley State Prison?"

"Yeah but he had life in prison, all the motivation in the world to infiltrate a cartel for the CIA. What would motivate this kid to go to Somalia for us?"

"It would be up to him. If he didn't want to go we could find somebody else, but I think I could talk him into it. Make life better for his mother and him, make sure he beats this rap!"

"Still he's only 14 years old!"

"We're still a few years off anyway, he will be old enough after fighting this case. When he get's out get's some training, I'll figure it out."

The CIA could send whomever wherever. All it took was the right person for the right mission. Brian ran the Somalian operation but Samuel had the contact's. Samuel would pull the strings necessary to help Brian get what he needed done.

*

Samuel arrived back at March on Friday morning. Pollard and Johnson patrolled the clear sky's of the southland with two predator drones.

"Hey Richardson! Good to see you back sir. How was the trip?" Johnson asked. His drone flew quietly over Balboa Island in Orange County. The vehicle pedestrian ferry could be seen moving slowly over slightly bumpy waters.

"Really good!" Samuel responded while putting a hand on Johnson's shoulder, leaning forward to view his screen. "Orange County is really beautiful. I miss California every time I leave. I did bring back some good news on a new toy for you guy's to play with."

"What is it?" Pollard asked.

"We'll have a meeting in a few minutes. First I need to brief Benson on a few things, is he here?"

"Yeah Benson's in the Pink Room, I mean Red Room. I still don't think I want to know what you guy's do in there all day." Pollard laughed as Johnson said this.

"It's really not that funny Pollard but regardless you'll be finding out what we do in the Red Room after I brief Benson." Samuel did his routine to enter the Red Room.

"Do you think we're going to get access to the Red Room?"
Pollard asked Johnson.

"I don't know but I'm not sure I want that chip injected
into my hand."

"I thought they made that part up?"

"No it's real man. Anyway's I got $200 saying I'll get
to Frisco before you?"

"Make it $250?" Pollard had a twenty minute head start.


*


"Samuel good to see you back brother! Any good news?"
Brian asked as his buddy boss entered the Red Room.

"Little bit. I got the top-2 (referring to the President
and CIA director) to allow for broader use of Trump Card."

"Really, who get's it now?"

"All CIA will now have access to it, with the edition
of the NSA, Secret Service, and FBI. A tech guy will be by today
to remove it from the Red Room and install it in central operations."

"What about my approval for Ghost? I should have clearance
I earned it!"

"Getting to that, I personally went over your application
with Thomas. His explanation is the same. No need for more people
to be in know about Ghost. There is a new program called "Core"
that has been revealed to me. My request for knowledge or access
to Core is pending. In the meantime until you receive clearance

for Ghost you nolonger have access to the Red Room. The tech guy will be here around noon. Make sure you are here so he can deactivate your chip."

"Sam this is bullshit! How can I effectively be second in command when I don't have access to the entire base? I'm really considering getting back into field work. I'm in the prime of my career and I'm sitting behind a desk."

"You remeber one thing Brian. We already put our lives on the line. You earned the right to sit on your ass making three hundred thousand a year. Why give it up for a youthful urge for an adrenaline rush? You're made Brian, Relax!"

"We did earn this, that you're right about. I just don't know if I am being rewarded enough."

"You will feel better when you see all of the good Trump Card will do now that the FBI can use it to solve crimes."

"You're right Sam, that should be great! The big city P.D.'s will be able to use it soon enough and the crime rates could really plunge."

They projected by 2006 New York and Los Angeles Police will have access to Trump Card. It will spread from there."

"I have a target for a possible O.T.R. in mind to join Ron in a few years." Brian quickly changed topic's.

"Who is it?" Samuel asked

"Remember the shooting we watched over 7th Street?"

"Yeah the wild west shoot-out at the dope house."

"Yeah that one. The kid Champ Washington who is charged

with the shooting may be a perfect O.T.R.. He is young like most
of the clan members. Also he is smart with a slight resemblance
to Ron in facial features."

"What about the kid's parents? I don't think you want
to kidnap the kid, even though we can?"

"His mother could be a problem but his father won't be.
His father is a man named Ky Washington. Currently serving a
life sentence based on shady L.A.P.D. and D.A. work from 96 to
97. Doesn't appear he committed the crime through my research.
We may be able to get him a reduced sentence, get the kid's mother
a big house. Get him out of juvenile hall?"

"Yeah well I can make what ever you need happen Brian.
Just let me know!"

Pollard and Johnson were excited to learn about Trump
Card and how they would both now be able to use it. The predator
drones would get a break. Agent Kim Bryant would be the last
to get briefed on Trump Card at the beginning of her shift.

Brian was not happy about losing access to the Red Room.
The thought of being able to use Trump Card with Kim on their
Somali mission perked him up a bit. Brian needed a way to meet
with Champ at the juvenile hall. He would figure out a way.

Chapter-7


Champ stepped out of his cell for the first time since
arriving to Group-2. It was one day after his first court appearance.
Champ strapped up his all white velcro shoes and walked with
his hands behind his back to the bench.

Rascal was seated to his right. Seated in a relaxed manner
as if too gangster to follow the rules of juvenile hall.

"Sit up straight! We do the same thing every morning."
The staff Mr. Henderson was looking at Rascal when he said this.

Rascal straightened up but kept a smug look on his face
without saying a word. Next to be released from his cell was
Chubby. He looked scared. Sharp breaths, shaky hands. Champ looked
Chubby in his eye's as he got closer. Ten feet, eight feet, six
feet, now four feet away Champ snapped to his feet. Champ moved
so fast Rascal jumped to his right even though Champ flew left
like a heat seeking missile toward Chubby.

Mr. Henderson rushed forward. Mr.A closed the door to cell 23 in the face of Silent from Temecula.

"Scan to Group-2!" Mr. A repeated into his radio three times. More staff would soon rush into Group-2 to break up the fight.

Before Chubby could bring his hands up to guard his face Champ landed a right to his nose, quick left to Chubby's right eye. running backward trying to fend off the enraged Champ, Chubby found his back against a hard railing. Champ stepped into Chubby's gut with his right leg. Chubby bent forward in pain. Champ lifted Chubby's body into a backflip over the railing with a powerful left uppercut to the jaw.

Chubby's face bled from right eye, nose, and lip as his body lay unconscious on his back. Champ turned his face to the right just in time to avoid a face full of Mr. Henderson's pepper spray. Champs eye's widened as the hulking Mr. Baker from Group-4 ran him over as if he still played safety for U.S.C..

"Stay down!" Champ was yelled at then cuffed behind his back. Before being escorted off to intake Champ could hear a nurse stating that an ambulance needed to be called for the kid still knocked out on the floor.

"Why did you beat that guy up?" Ms. Beltran the Supervisor asked Champ as she escorted him to intake.

"It's a long story lady, I don't think you want to hear it."

The noesy supervisor did in fact want to hear it. Champ would not feed her any information. Her body was already a sloppy fat that could explode from her stretch pants at anytime. But the concern here was that her air baloon shaped head would pop if she thought to hard about anything.

Champ received a pepper spray shower even though he was not sprayed. Back to cell 21 he was taken. Champ was assigned another 24 hour lockdown with the warning of a 72 hour lockdown if he kept it up.

"Your violence will not be tolerated here Washington. I will have you in shackles everytime you leave your cell." This promise was made by large and incharge Ms. Beltran.

Champ did not wish upon himself the cruelty of 24 hour lockdowns but vise versa he felt the need to express his anger on the right person. Later in the day while bouncing a dry rolled up ball of toilet paper off of the wall, two letters slid under his door.

The first letter was from his beloved mother who mailed one to him 7 days a week. The second letter made Champs heart bumb up and down. He excitedly read and re-read the name on the envelope enjoying the feeling he got each time. Sofia! His angel. Her address read Utah? He hurried to open the letter to find out what the change ment. He read slowly.

'Dear Champ,
        I miss you so much! I cry every night thinking about you Champ. I want to help you so bad but I don't know what to do? I saw the newspaper and I know it's wrong. I was there Champ. I can tell them you didn't do anything. Maybe your mom can move here when you get out? My mother told me the shooting on 7th Street has gotten worse. They found Michael the kid from our history class dead in the alley behind a dumpster. Somebody shot him. That's really scary so I am grateful to be away from that. I just want you to get away too! Don't go back there Champ it's dangerous! Promise me you'll make your mom move you? It's hard enough that your in there. I miss and love you! Be good and keep your head up!
                Love,
                    Sofia'

Champ felt weightless after reading Sofia's letter. Like he could float away to Heaven after knowing his angel loved and cared about him. If anger could have made him a big green monster that could break down his cell walls and giant step his way to Utah he could not have done it. Happiness was so prevalent withen him that anger was forced to a microscopic part of his brain. Champ felt it impossible to ever get angry again after reading such a letter. He blocked out the news about Michael.

Not being allowed to have writing material in their cells Champ was lucky enough to have a piece of pencil lead and a sheet of writing paper. He used his finger nail to dig the pencil lead from the window seal. Folding his mattress he wrote using the slab of concrete as a desk. Champ wrote Sofia a page long letter in responce. He said, "Don't worry about nothing!" Champ assured Sofia he was okay and would go to see her in Utah as soon as he got out. On the back of the letter Champ did something he had never done before. He wrote Sofia a poem to express his feelings. It was titled and written as such:

"Our Poem:Written For You"
I would love to see the smile I bring,
To dub you with a crystal whiter than light ring,
Happiness short of what life brings,
Be the other half see your pearly whites gleam,
No watch I know what the time is,
Your grin is forever priceless,
Flush money it can't buy it,
Words roaring louder than a lion,
Without yours I was dying,
Your letter was honest I'm now blinded,
So much light in truth I'm now finding,
Your words co-signing,
Love for you my highness,
If I could just rewind this,
I'll show you what life is,
Would we ever find a gift,
Full of poems to make us rich,
Big'ol home for the kids,
Sticks and stones may break my ribs,
Surely more than positive,
I would live to make it big,
Just to see you smile again,
God made us forever friends,
This is just where it begins.

*

Friday Night Lights! Well the night was Friday. There
were lights on the 15 foot walls around the juvenile halls big
field. Flag football would be played but everybody out here knew
it was more than that. The passion on this field would never
be in the history books. The only columns these kid's would be
getting in the papers is that they were convicted or sentenced
to a life time in prison for their murders, robberies, or association
to such crimes.

Four teams of five was how it was played. The winning
team got the spoils on Saturday. Pizza or hot wings depending
on what Mr. Gomez wanted to eat. It was Mr. Gomez who came up
with Friday Night Lights for the kid's. He knew only two of the
twenty would avoid prison. Eighteen of them were on their way
to one of Californias 33 big houses.

Champ was put on the same team as Chubby for a reason.
Mr. Gomez wanted them to work as a team. Work together instead
of fighting. Champ and Chubby were the only one's who knew why
they fought. They weren't going to tell on each other even though
Champ would benefit from it.

Raw Dog lost two teamates to the county jail so Champ
and Chubby were added to his team. They joined Fat Boy Jason,
and Smash-G to form team 1. Team 2 was Duce's team. His teammates
were Blacky, Silent, Frog, and Midget.

Team 3 was Franks. He had Rascal, Flaco, Spider, and Y.G..

Adam was the best quarterback of the bunch and he had
the best running back in Shorty and best wide receiver in Dino.
All Shadow and Daffy had to do was put up a two man block and
team 4 was primed to expand their five week win streak to six.

Team 1 played team 2 first. Each game set for 30 minutes. Smash-G kicked the ball off and Midget from Los Angeles received it. Midget ran behind his blockers until contact was made. He split left but Raw Dog was there to force him out of bounds.

Blacky was quarterback, Silent blocked, Midget was the back with Duce, and Frog split wide.

Raw Dog and Smash-G covered the coners while Jason rushed. Champ and Chubby stood on opposite sides watching for a run. Despite playing for the same team they still did not like each other. The stares they shot each other could have killed a lessor man.

"Set Hike!" Blacky took 3 steps back. Jason rushed into Silent pushing him backwards. Blacky tossed the ball to Midget who was quickly run over by Chubby. This may have been called flag football but every kid knew it was hit first pull flag later.

This really got Mr. Gomez blood pumping. He paced the sideline as the official Ref often yelling, "Hit sombody!"

His coworker Ms. Pixley enjoyed the games just as well. Only more quietly from the opposite sideline.

Team 2 was pushed further away from the orange cone that marked first down when Blacky tucked the ball to run with it. Champ pulled Blacky's flag with no contact. He got an earful from Mr. Gomez, "Why didn't you hit him? This ain't sissy ball, I want to see you hit somebody!"

"He's too scared to hit me!" Blacky taunted while grinning at Champ.

Champ didn't respond verbally. He couldn't get angry. His mind wouldn't let him. He did want to hit Blacky, but only to prove that he could and wasn't scared.

With 3rd and long Blacky hiked the ball taking his normal
three steps back. He was looking down field when Champ caught
him from his blindside. Champ lowered his shoulder and made contact
with Blacky's ribs. The ball flew out of his hands as he went
down in pain.

Mr. Gomez blew his whistle. "Illegal rush, automatic first
down!" Mr. Gomez looked down at Blacky. "Are you okay son? Can
you still play?"

"Naw! This shit hurts, I feel like my ribs are broken!"

"Sit on the sideline. When we go in I will call the nurse
to see you. Tell her you fell. I saw you fall." Blacky was helped
to the sideline. "Adam come in the game!" Mr.Gomez called him
in as a replacement. Adam would still play for his team but if
his teams were to play in the final game somebody else would
be called upon to replace Blacky.

On 1st down Adam hit Duce in the end zone over Smash-G
for a touchdown. Smash-G blamed Champ and by the surprise of
everybody Chubby spoke up for him. "It's you slow ass fault!
Champs doing his job now do yours!"

"Nigga I'll whip yo ass!" Smash-G marched for Chubby.

"Stop crying to each other! I'm not going to let either
of you mess my food up! Now let's get a touchdown!" Raw Dog stepped
between the two and defused the situation.

They agreed to give Raw Dog the kickoff because he was
the fastest. Everyone else would block. It was a shorter than
assumed kickoff and the ball fell into the hands of Chubby. Instead
of pitching the ball back to Raw Dog as planned Chubby ran forward.
His team watched in disgust as Chubby wobbled forward with no
blockers. Champ chuckled thinking it was funny Chubby defied
the teams wishes.

With all of the misguided confidence in the world Chubby refusing to go left or right ran into the duo of Duce and Adam. Chubby was lifted and tossed backward by the healthy youngsters. The ball was in the air before Chubby's ass hit the ground. Midget caught the ball and sped to the end zone. Cubby's teammates were too busy laughing at him. Midget scored to make the game 14-0. Raw Dog forfeited the game for his team. They took a seat on the sideline and watched the next two games.

Adam led his team to glory in a tuff 28-21 victory. The final game was a blowout. Frank played for the injured Blacky but didn't matter. Adam put on his best Payton Manning impersonation and won the food with a 49-0 shutout. Champ felt he would never get the Saturday special as long as Adam was playing. He was on a six week winning streak with over a dozen victories. Champ lied to himself with thoughts of,'I don't like pizza and hot wings anyway!' Yes he did.

Champ went to his arraignment in adult court. Lazy sat with the county jail inmates who wore orange. Champ wore a yellow jumpsuit an sat separately from the county jail inmates. When Champs case was called Lazy was named as his codefendant. At visiting champs mother Linda told Champ he would be getting a public defender for an attorney.

"Champ please don't punch anybody, their never going to let you out if you act violent." Linda pleaded with her son.

Champ apologized to his mother for punching his lawyer. He assured her he would never do anything of the sort again. The new attorney informed Champ that she needed time to go over the Distric Attorney's discovery before she would know the details of his case. For now they would plead not guilty and postpone setting a preliminary hearing date for a month.

Champ could not believe he had to wait another month to come back to court. He was ready to go to trial now! Why wouldn't

he be. He didn't do anything. Champ had to accept his situation.
There was nothing he could do about it except go with the flow.
The lawyer woman told him she would visit within the next month,
go over the case with him and ask questions. Champ asked about
bail. She said not today but she would look into it for their
next court date. Champ did not make his bed, but he sure had
to lie in it.

A week after Champs arraignment a surprise slid under
his cell door. "Prison mail!" Ms. Beltran said as she slid a
letter under his door. All mail from prison was reviewed by a
supervisor before being passed out. "You're lucky I got the letter.
Another supervisor would have sent it back. When you write make
sure you tell him not to write stuff like that or we may not
give you his letters."

"What's it say?" Champ asked.

"Read it." Ms. Big Beltran rumbled away from his door.

Never before has Champ received a letter directly from
his father. The letters sent to his mother had quick notes in
each for Champ. The likes of, 'Stay out of trouble son, stay
in school. Take care of your mother.' This was new. An eight
page letter written to him by a father he last seen through the
visiting glass of the L.A. county jail in 1997. Champ was 8 years
old.

Champ read his fathers letter slowly. It was full of tuff
advice about how not to let a public defender screw him over.

'Fight for yourself Champ! You are a born winner! That's
why I named you Champ. You have to believe in yourself. All these
devils want to do is put you in a big concrete casket like your
ol'pops. Your just a kid Champ. Push for a speedy trial, they
can't deny you. If you don't push they will age you. You won't
see a jury until you're 19, 20 years old. A jury won't feel any

sympathy for you. Push Champ, Fight!' Champs father went on in
his letter to tell his story.

\*

Ky Washington was 37 years old when he was sent to prison
for the rest of his life. Twelve years removed from his last
and first incarceration in the California Youth Authority. This
was Ky's first time in the county jail. Now prison.

Being stripped of all underwear all you wore was an orange
county jail jumpsuit. At mid-night you are rounded up with the
other prison bound inmates and left in a cold holding tank. By
3a.m. the bus leaves the L.A. county jail for North Kern State
Prison's reception center. The 5 freeway north to the 99 freeway
north. Three hours into the bus ride you exit to the small town
of Delano. You see the tall prison lights. Your home. Shuffled
off of the prison bus one by one. It's your turn. It's freezing!
You shiver. You're told to strip at the door. You wonder if you
heard the officer correctly?

It's winter. Ice is visible on the windows. You step just
inside of the wide door. It does not feel like inside. You remove
the counties jumpsuit and flip flops. Toss them in bins on the
wall to your left. The sheriff's will be taking them back to
the county for the next batch of inmates. You feel the freezing
air at your naked back. There is a male correctional officer
standing infront of you. He barks commands at you like you would
a dog. You're being searched in the freezing ass doorway. This
is bullshit!

You are told to open your mouth. Lift up your tongue.
At this very moment the office door five feet infront of you
open's. A woman correctinal officer stands and looks confused
for a moment. You are not bothered by the fact that she is staring

Chapter 7 | 107

at your hanging penis. Your pissed to see her all cozy and warm in a puffy jacket while your naked skins war with the chilling wind is a losing one. You are told to lift your testicles. You are now visibly shaking. It's cold. The female officer walks away just as you are instructed to squat and cough.

You're now directed to enter further into the receiving area of the prison. You're happy to be away from the open door but you still weren't given any clothes. You are still naked. You now face the biggest rounded table you will ever see. It's a giant circle with lot's of correctional officer duties taking place withen it's circumference. You don't know whether to go left or right. You pick left because you see a metal detector and assume you have to walk through it.

As you confused and nakedly walk you see a chubby puddgy little correctional officer lady sitting in a chair arms crossed legs open. You look at her but she won't meet your eye's. She is preoccupied. You once again have a stranger woman looking at what makes you a man. How many penises has she seen this morning? Four different counties with four different buses each filled with forty different people. That's 160 sausages she's visually had for breakfast this morning. You wonder how she would rank you. Top ten? Maybe nine? Yeah she likes you. The darker green of her jumpsuit between her legs makes you wonder if she has grown moist? Could a maxi-pad with wings have helped conceal her excitement?

You pass through the metal detector and see a line of naked dudes infront of you. Slowly one by one they're being handed a single pair of 3X boxers. The inmate passing out the boxers must have held the least respected job in all of prison. You hurry to slip on the underwear and almost take a tumble into your new cold holding tank. The boxers are too big but you hold them to your waist. This will be the only thing you get to wear until the afternoon. You grab your knees to try and warm, wondering what has just happened to you.

You feel as if you have just been through a traumatic situation. The younger you are, the worse. Humiliated and naked as Jews must have felt as they were shaved and marched into the incinerators. Your incenerator was the freezing holding tank where your mind freaks as it comes to the realization that you have now entered a world that you would nolonger have a chance at leaving. Life ment Life! Similar  is the stubborn cow who fights for his existence at the slaughterhouse. At least the cows put up a fight. You simply walk to your demise. Naked!

Chapter-8


Ky Washington was by no means a saint. He was a bitter man who grew more violent with his sentence. While at North Kern State Prison he solidified his standing as a high ranking member of his crip gang. Two beatings of rival gang members and a staff assault earned Ky a five year S.H.U. program. (S.H.U.-is a Security Housing Unit).

Arriving to Pelican Bay State Prison in 1997 Ky would serve his S.H.U. term here. Stepping off of the prison bus he was told to look straight up at the sky without looking down. This was the most violent prison for the most violent inmates. You were treated like it. Ky spent five years on 23 hour lockdown, in what was called C-yard. This was not a yard. Just a large building of cells. One half known as C, the other as D.

Ky had the same seven neighbors for years. All validated prison gang members with life sentences. To get out of the S.H.U. they would have to rat on their fellow gang members. Something they refused to do. Literally these men were dead six feet

deep in a coffin but still breathing. The hour out of their cell
daily gave for a bit of breathing room. Fourteen steps to the
small yard. Tiny concrete entrapment with a tinted screen for
a roof. A camera watched your body slighty move around the 12
by 6 foot environment. This area you got for an hour was not
for your body to escape. It was for your mind.

Five years without a window to see through or a person
to punch changed Ky just enough that he became a religious person.
In 2002 Ky was released to Pelican Bay's B-yard. Ky would now
be allowed to move around and mingle with the general population.
Ky was 40 years old and his gang looked to him as an O.G.. Ky
read the Koran less and less with the more freedom and power
he was gaining on the yard.

Within in a year by the beginning of 2003 the yard was
his. Anything involving a crip Ky was responsible for. If Ky
said ride you would ride, if Ky said die you died! When a crip
disrespected a southern Mexican it was Ky's responsibility to
defuse the situation before it got out of hand. The Mexicans
explained to Ky that if he got the disrespectful crip off of
the yard it would solve the issue. They didn't care how the Black's
did it, just as long as they got rid of the guy.

Ky had a lot of pride. The 20 year old crip in question
was the son of his good friend. He informed everybody that the
man could stay. This angered more than half of the crip's on
the yard.

The Mexicans were furious! Fate? Destiny? It's hard to
beat. As if by fate and destiny on the same Friday morning during
the month of March that Champ was surrounded by mexicans and
stabbed, Ky found himself in the same situation.

It was morning yard release, out of the 70 Blacks that
could have come to yard, only Ky and 17 other Blacks did. All
80 Mexicans allowed to come out that morning were on the yard.

The 20 year old crip who started this distubance had conveniently left the yard a day earlier. He told a correctional officer that he feard for his life. Ky regretted ever standing up for him.

When the knives came out only one side had them. The Mexicans. Ky and five other crips tried to fight. They paid for their stubbornness with various stab wounds. Twelve Crips ran for the gate under the gunners tower. The insane Mexicans ran through the gunners bullets to stab the fearful Blacks. It was a mess! The correctional officers did not enter the yard until 40 minutes into the one sided riot.

Ky lay bloodied in the middle of the yard. Stabbed 47 times he clung to life but could not move. He hung on to consciousness, Mexicans moved passed him. No need to stab something that already looked dead.

Ky woke up in the prison infirmary. He was in a cell by himself. So much pain he wished he died instead of surviving. His body seemed wrapped up from head to toe. Ky passed out!

Ky woke up to the sound of a correctional officers key's jingling. A nurse was in his single man infirmary cell. Ky was unconscious for a week but finally he was back to reality. Ky disbelieved the number of time's he was stabbed. 47! Not possible he thought.

Ky was still in the infirmary when he sent Champ the 8-page letter. Linda wrote to inform him of what happened to their son. Linda begged Ky to write Champ and give him some advice on how to deal with his situation.

Ky felt more pain for his son than he did in his violated body. After writing the letter to his son he swung his leg's over the side of his infirmary bed. Lowering himself down in his wheelchair, Ky rolled over to the cell door to slip the letter in the tray slot where it would be picked up by a c.o. to be mailed.

mailed out. Ky cried. He was paralyzed from the waist down.

*

Champ cried after reading his fathers letter. He dug the pencil lead from the window seal. He wrote a two page letter in response and finished his letter off with a poem.

'We're Champions'

I'm proud to be your youngin,
Have you as my dad,
These times are full of suffering,
We're not getting mad,
Stronger than most of men,
What Cain and Able should have been,
Humble to our next of kin,
Even if their Mexican,
No doubt we're the best of men,
What the Fed's should have been,
Sending us to the Pen,
Because the color of our skin,
But we're not getting back at um,
Harass and attacking them,
We relax sit back,
We're the Champions,
I'm Champ you're Ky Washington,
In the mirror you look back at me,
Thanks for that dad,
Now I will forever live happily...'

Champs brain was filled to capacity with as much stress as he could take. Time slowed to a crawl. The pressure a 14 year old feels while being helplessly locked in a cell with the possibility of it lasting a life time, is like trying to stop an Atomic Bomb by covering it with a glass dome. You're going to shatter! Champ broke down and cried under the cover of his blankets at night. During the day nobody could tell Champ was feeling so depressed.

A week before his court date Champ was called for an attorney visit. Champ heard nothing from his lawyer the entire month. He was anxious. Standing to greet Champ was a fit looking white man in a expensive suit.

"Your not my lawyer." Champ looked leery of the man. His lawyer was a woman.

"No, your absolutely right Champ. But I am here to help you."

"Help me? I don't need help from the police. Your help is why I'm here!"

"No, no, I'm not the police Champ. I saw what happened that day on 7th Street. I want to help you out."

"Who are you?"

"Just a guy with lot's of friends. Please have a seat."

Champ sat across from the man.

"Champ you are a very smart kid. I've personally gone over your school records. I'm impressed! Straight A's your whole 7th grade, about to repeat that in the 8th. Then Macho and his friends jump you on your way to school messing your life up. The girl, you never mentioned the girl to the authorities. I really respect loyalty in a person. That's what my business is all about. Loyalty. Except in my world you have to be loyal to our nation. Do what's best for the United States."

"Look man I don't know what kind of game you're playing with me. I wasn't with any girl! I'll see you in trial, and I'm going to win!" Champ barked at the man with more frustration than anger.

"Calm down Champ. I'm not going to be at anybody's trial, it's not my thing. And I like you protecting Sofia, even at the expense of your own freedom. That's rare in a 14 year old. I would not be here if I couldn't help you or you help me at the same time."

At the mention of Sofia's name Champ tensed.'Nobody knew that she was there. Maybe she contacted this man?' Champ thought.

"I don't believe too much of what anybody's been saying lately. I just want to know who are you and why did you come to visit me? What do you want from me?"

"Those are great questions. What I am about to tell you about myself you cannot repeat to anybody else. If you do we will no longer have an agreement. I will find another person just like you. Nobody will believe somebody who's a convicted murderer serving life in prison."

"I'm not a murderer!" Champ spouted.

"I know that Champ, but if you take this to a jury without my help they're going to convict you. Riverside County currently hold's a 97% conviction rating. The nations highest! You need me. Now let me explain. My name is Brian Benson. I work for the CIA. I'm in charge of a covert operation that you would be perfect for. You will learn much more about this when you're released. If you agree to work for us this is what we will do. One: you go home, beat your case guaranteed. You could represent yourself and still win. Two: You could pick a place for you and your mother to live. She retires with a hundred grand every year. She's set for life. Your father. Get him from a life without parole sentence to a 15 year term. He'll be out in another 7 years. You personally will make five hundred thousand yearly while you are in the field. When the mission's over you can work for the Agency full-time or go off on your own. Free to live however you want."

"Despite how crazy this all sounds why would you need me? I'm only 14, what can I do for you?"

Brian stood, "Champ you can help make the World a safer place. Spend some time to think this over. If you don't tell anybody about what I told you, I will be back to see you in a

few months. Stay out of trouble, and oh yeah," Said with a chuckle.
"Work on your football skill's. Your letting that other team
whoop you every week!" Brian reached for the door to leave.

"Wait, why a few months? Why not get me out today?" Champ
stopped him with his question; from leaving the confidential
attorney visiting room.

"Important things take time Champ. Just have patience."
Brian put on his sunglasses and walked out of the visiting room.
Brian thanked the lone juvenile hall staff member. The Sun was
shining. Picture perfect day in the French Valley, Murrieta
California. Brian wondered if he really was doing the young Champ
a favor. A life of oppressive years in prison or a violent tour
of duty in Samolia for a few years? Yes he really was trying
to do the kid a favor.

*

Champ spent the next two years in Juvenile Hall. Each
court date was set two months apart from each other. A total
of 15 court dates after his first one the prosecutor finally
announced that the State was ready to proceed to trial. Champs
invocation of his right to a speedy trial fell upon deaf ears.
Nobody cared or suffered except Champ and his mother.

A deal had to be reached with Lazy. He would plead guilty
to 1 count of manslaughter for a total term of 12 years in State
Prison. Champ faced a total of 70 years to life in prison if
convicted on all counts against him.

Champ had not heard from the man claiming to be CIA since
his one and only visit 2 years ago. None the less he never spoke
of the visit hoping just in case that what the man said was true.
He wished it was true. His gut told him whatever Lazy had to

say on the stand was going to cost him his freedom. It was the summer of 2005. The lady representing Champ was a flop. She was 0-for-5 in her murder trial career.

Champ wanted to represent himself but the 16 year old lacked the knowledge. The day before jury selection there was a surprise visitor for Champ at the juvenile hall. Champ wanted to sceam out in excitement when he saw Brian waiting in the attorney visiting room. Keeping his composer Champ took a seat across from Brian.

"Where have you been at man?" Champ asked.

"Hey looks like you're glad to see me, I had to wait to see how you would fair with the information I gave you."

"Two years! Really? You said a few months?"

"I know what you mean Champ, it's a long time to wait. I personally would like to get you out of here as soon as possible. I just need you to agree to help your Country. Regardless of danger or what you may be called upon to do to others. Country first! No questions asked!"

"What if I go to trial without your help and beat my case?"

"We both know you will lose with Lazy pointing the finger at you. What do you say Champ are you in or are you out? You can't be both!"

"When will I be out of here?"

"Tomorrow!"

"I'm in!" Champ responded.

*

The Distric Attorney was furious when his boss informed him to drop the Washington case. Over two years of hard work down the drain. The deal Lazy was given would now be revoked as there was no longer anybody to testify against. Therefore a deal would no longer be necessary. That morning in court the D.A. announced it was dropping it's case against Mr. Washington and refiling those charges against Mr. Coleman, A.K.A. Lazy. Sure to spend the rest of his life in prison was Lazy who gave one too many statements. Those statements would now be used to convict him of murder for his dead brother, and three attempted murders for the other victims. The Felony Murder Rule worked magic for the D.A.'s office. If you are there you are guilty! Guaranteed!

Champ was now 6 foot 1 and 190-pounds. Healthy as ever and finally free! He breathed in deeply as he hugged his mother in front of the juvenile hall.

"You're home baby, you're home! I can't believe it's really happening!" Linda cried. She has dreamed of this moment for 2 years.

"I love you so much mom! We really need to get away from here, I think I'm going to throw up." Champ realized he never told his mother about the CIA or deal he made in exchange for his freedom.

"Come on baby let's get in the car. Roll your window down to get some air." Linda said.

The car was the same red Honda Civic. Scratches and dents from over the years were ignored. One hub cap three blackened rims.

"Champ my prayers were answered! God had to have a hand in this! We're free! It feel's so good!" The Honda was moving slowly down a jam packed Temecula street toward the 215 freeway.

"I'm happy too mom!" Champ had a few tears of joy coming down his cheek, as he turned the knobs of the car radio. Champ put the radio on 99.1 KGGI. His favorite radio station besides K-DAY.

"Yumm Del-Taco! Can we get some?" Champ longed for some fast food, or free man food.

"We can have whatever you want Champ. We'll go in and eat!"

"Good! I haven't been in a restaurant for so long I might faint!"

The pair took a table. Macho burrito's, diet Coke for Linda, Sprite for Champ.

"Mom I made this deal with this guy to get out of prison."

"Guy? What guy? You're silly. They dropped your case Champ."

"No mom I'm serious. I made a deal for all of us. You dad and me. I get out of jail, you get a big house with a hundred thousand dollar a year retirement. Dad only has to do seven more years in prison."

"What? I really don't believe why somebody would do all of that. How would they and what's in it for them?"

"Look mom this guy came to see me and," Champ was cut off by his mothers cell phone ringing.

"Hold on a second Champ." Linda answered her phone. "Hello!"

"Hi Ms. Washington my name is Brian Benson, I would like to speak with your son?"

"My son? Well who the fuck are you calling to speak with my son? This is my phone! Who gave you this number?" Linda was angery at the man on the phone but stared at Champ wondering if he was the one to give out her number?

"Who is it mom?" Champ asked.

"Linda it is very important that you let me speak with Champ. I know you're confused but you will be given some details shortly."

Linda slowly handed her son the phone saying, "You better start speaking up! I'm your mother, you don't keep secrets from me!"

"Hello?" Champ spoke into the phones receiver.

"Hey Champ your doing a really good job buddy! I'm just calling to give you a heads up on what will be taking place."

"Okay but how did you get my mothers phone number, she's pissed."

"I'm the real deal Champ! Now you can tell your mother you're going on a mission for the L.D.S. church. You will be sent to spain to spread the book of Mormon. Why's, what's, and how's don't matter. Ask her to pick a place to live and there will be one-hundred G's waiting for her in a safe in the master bedroom."

"Okay I understand that part but how long do I have before you need me?"

"I'm going to have you on a plane bound for Utah tonight

Champ. While you are at the Missionary Training Center in Utah
you will be able to write to your mother but that's it. At the
M.T.C. you will learn everything you need to know about the country
you will be heading to. You will study the language and customs
of the people. It's a three month process after which you'll
get three months of training at one of our training facilities."

"I can't leave today! I couldn't do that to my mother.
You have to at least give me a week?"

"A week we don't have!" Brian said.

"What is this? Give me the phone Champ!" Linda demandingly
took the phone from her son.

"This is what it is! Leave us alone and don't ever call
this number again!" Linda hung up the phone. "Let's go Champ!"

They both got into the red Honda Civic.

At the March Base Brian had just been hung up on. "Samuel
this kid's mom is not having it. I need to go over there and
smooth this over." Brian said.

"What are you going to tell her?" Asked Samuel.

"Probably a crazy story that I represent the powerful
L.D.S. church and that we feel they are the choosen one's!"

"Is it really that bad Brian?"

"The truth never works. You figure the spoils alone would
convince her this is right?"

"Yeah the mother son thing is tricky! You can get a guy
out of prison, but you can't get him out of the arm's of his
mother! Well good luck Brian." Samuel walked over to the Red

Room to enter.

"Yeah thank you Sam!" Brian stepped into the elevator
to leave. He was going to drive to 6th Street and try to perform
a miracle.

The red Honda Civic exited the 215 freeway at 4th Street.
The Gateway to downtown Perris.

Champ explained to his mother what he had been directed
to over the phone.

"Ain't no damn church got you out of prison Champ! And
they are damn sure not going to make you leave me!"

"They'll get you a house and money!"

"Ha ha that's the funniest thing I ever heard!" Linda
parked in the alley next to their apartment.

"This is the only piece of shit home we'll ever have Honey."
Linda turned the car off grabbed her purse and stepped from the
car.

Champ had yet to open his door when an explosion sent
red through the open drivers side door hurling in his direction!
Blood and chunks of his mothers skull stung his face and arm's!
He wiped blood from his eye's. Something was in his mouth? Champ
spit it on the dashboard. It was an ear with his mothers earring
still in place! Champ looked to his left as he opened his door.
His mothers head was missing and her body still clad in a perfect
dress was twisted in a pool of blood. Champ fainted through the
open passenger side door.

## Chapter-9


Champ awoke to find his face on the dirty pavement. Drool and blood on the side of his face. Buggers and snot came when Champ began wailing in agony for the fate of his mother. The grill to an all black B.M.W. stopped in his face. Champ wanted to die. Join his mother to make her happy.

"Champ get up!" A voice called. "We have to get you away from here!"

Champ lay limp as he let the man drag him to the backseat of the spotless B.M.W. Brian gave the scene a look over. No gunner in sight but Linda's head was missing. Brian got into his B.M.W., sped to D Street and entered the freeway.

Brian wondered if the local gang's had slain Champs mother as retaliation against him? Brian got a good look at Linda's body and the amount of splattered blood. He didn't know of any ammo or weapon the street thug's had that would explode a persons head as if a stick of dynamite had gone off. Brian drove Champ to his apartment. The kid was a wreck.

*

Agent Ron Davis was expecting a new agent to join him
in 6 months. Brian was trying to make that happen and not a day
late. Despite what just occurred Brian still planned to have
Champ on a plane to Utah that night. The undercover CIA agent
who worked as a teacher at the missionary training center in
Provo was also a Psychologist. He could take care of Champ.

Champ stood in the shower with his head propped against
the corner. He watched the water flow down the drain. It represented
his life. Going down the drain in a hurry! Champ filled his mouth
with water gagging it down the drain. Champ fell to his knees
letting the water shower his back. 'Why my mother?' He cried.
The beast within him was growing with the images of his dead
mother. Two machine guns to level the entire block to it's foundation
6th and 7th Street reduced to rubble by a crazed man and his bloody
tears. 'I love and miss you.' Where was this thought coming from?
The words 'I miss and love you' interrupted all of Champs hellish
thoughts. He could hear Sofia's voice clear as day in his head.
Utah! She was living with family in Utah. Brian said something
about sending him to Utah? Champs sudden urge to see Sofia was
overwhelming.

Champ burst through the bathroom door dressed in Brian's
hand me downs. Brian slammed his laptop closed and rose from
the couch. "Champ what happened? What do you remeber?"

"Nothing but my mothers head exploding. You're the damn
CIA! I need you to find out who did this! I'll go through your
training and work for you guy's but my terms need to be met!"

"What are your terms Champ?"

"First and most important thing I need for you to do is find out who killed my mother? Second my father doesn't spend another year in prison, he's out by Christmas. Now you said something about Utah? Okay I want to go to Utah but I need to see somebody there."

"Is that person Sofia?"

"How do you know about her?" Champ asked.

"We monitor stuff like phone calls and mail. I saw her letters to you."

"Did you read my mail?"

"No, no, I didn't care to read your mail, just kept note of address."

"What is it Brian, do we have a deal?"

"I can meet your terms. Your plane leaves at 3p.m. from across the street."

"Across the street? Where are we?"

"Take a look." Brian opened his front door and they stepped onto his balcony which looked out towards the March Air Reserve Base main runway.

"We're in Moreno Valley. This is the Air Force Base." Champ stated.

"That's right you get your own personal flight to Salt Lake City on a cargo plane." Brian said.

\*

Champ buckled up and sat behind the Pilots seat. Never flying in his entire life this was a spiritual experience for him. The Pilot didn't speak to Champ. He didn't need them to. The G-force held Champ to the back of his seat on take off. The windows large and clear in the cockpit. Moreno Valley under him, Box Springs to his left with the large M (for Moreno Valley) on the mountaintop fast appoaching. Champ wondered if this was how his mother felt as she was lifted by God to Heaven?

*

2005 was the start of Juan Carlos's political career. He was a 27 year old stud in Utah's world of Mormon politics. His 22 year old girlfriend was pregnant with his first child. Jennifer Atkif moved from her home in Perris California after graduating high school to be with Juan. The pregnancy of Jennifer was kept a secret by having her live with her mother in Riverside. Having a baby out of wedlock was taboo in Utah. One would have to move to Canada to escape the ridicule from such an act. A politician may be hung in public fashion in front of a loud cheering audience.

After giving birth Jennifer would return to Utah to marry Juan Carlos. Their first born would have to be forgotten as if he did not exist to spare Juan Carlos his political career. Forgotten but still loved the child would be. Jennifer's mother Colleen had lost both of her children for different reasons. Her daughter to the charm of Juan Carlos and the L.D.S. church. Colleen's 16 year old son Shawn was incarcerated two months passed his 15th birthday. He faced life in prison after being around a burglary that resulted in the homeowners beating death. His none guilt was irrelevant faced with a 97% chance at being found guilty.

Colleen was more than happy to have another baby to raise. She was given permission to name her grandson. Jackson was born on Independence Day. July 4th, 2005.

Jennifer returned to Utah. Juan's office in Provo was lavish. Nicer than the Governor's office. Pictures of Juan and his soon to be wife on his desk with paper weights and stacks of legislation paperwork. On the wall behind Juan Carlos's chair next to the huge bulletproof window (that appeared as only a thin layer of clear glass) was what people remembered after leaving this office. There was a dozen pictures with Juan Carlos stading next to the most powerful men on Earth. The U.S., Chinese, and Russian presidents. Current heads of the European Union, African Union, and Arab League.

Juan's sheer charm was overwhelming to everbody he met. World leaders yearned to know this man. The people of Utah wanted Juan as their Governor but he refused to run in an election for top man in the State. He wanted to win the White House one day and he felt his best chance was running as a long term Senator from Utah. Strong Mormon tie's but more open-minded for the American people.

Alone in Juan's office Jennifer and him spoke. "What did she name him? Juan asked.

"Jackson! I can't believe we lost our first child because of politics." Jennifer looked sad toward Juan.

"It's okay baby, your mother will take good care of him. Whenever she need's money for him I'll supply it. He couldn't ask for a better life."

"That HE is my baby Juan! I feel so guilty. It should have never happened like this."

"We lost OUR child! It's going to take some time but when we realize he was not ment for us we will feel better. You're marrying the future president baby. Cheer up!"

"I guess you're right Juan. Nobody can resist you."

"That's the Jennifer I know. Be my rock and we will change the World!"

"You are the World honey!" Jennifer leaned in to kiss her man.

*

Champ didn't know where he was when the plane landed and he exited. He left the same way he boarded the plane through the back ramp that came down from the planes backside.

Dr. Lance Von was a teacher at the Missionary Training Center who was also employed by the CIA. Dr. Von waited for Champ at the bottom of the ramp with his all white Lexus jeep conveniently parked up close to it.

"Hi Champ! Nice to meet you." Said with a smile, "Let's get in my jeep, it's chilly out here." Dr. Von went for his drivers side door.

"My names Champ Washington. Where are we?" It was quiet and warm inside of the Lexus.

"I know your name Champ. Brian sent me a file on you. And we are in Utah. Nobody told you?"

"I knew where I was going but where am I at in Utah? Is this a military base?"

"No, this is just a private airfield we use. We are only 20 minutes outside of Provo."

"What did you say your name was?"

"My name is Dr. Lance Von, but you can call me Mr. Von.
All of the students at the M.T.C. do."

"Where am I going, and what do I need to do?" Asked Champ
eager to know.

"Have you ever heard of a place called Somalia?"

"Yeah, the Horn of Africa." Champ responded.

"Yes. Smart kid!"

"I read the World Almanac a few times while I was in juvenile
hall."

"That's a good thing Champ. While you will be staying at
the M.T.C., Missionary Training Center, I will teach you the
language and customs of the Somali people. The only thing I was
told was to teach you how to live in Somalia. I don't know what
you will be doing, or if you're going to Somalia at all. You
will share a room with other guy's at the M.T.C.. Your name is
Mark Young. You are 20 years old from Canyon Lake California.
You don't like to talk much, so don't. You will be in my class
where I teach Arabic for the people the church is sending to
Jordan. Pay attention because the customs are similar. After
class I'll teach you more appropriate Somali Arabic. Everybody
will assume you are going to Jordan with them. Feed into it."

"Mr. Von this is all moving way too fast! My name is Mark
now? I'm 20? I don't even look 20!"

"Your are going to be fine Champ. It will only take you
a day or two to get comfortable. You have two day's to report
to the M.T.C.. You have a hotel room, shopping mall across the
street, get some clothes for yourself." Mr. Von handed Champ

a drivers licence under the name Mark Young with a stack of $100
bills. "Eat what you want, see who you want, do what you want.
Just don't buy a car and try to drive to Vegas. Brian will find
you wherever you are."

Mr. Von gave Champ a manila envelope with all he needed
to know about his identity inside of it.

"So your just going to leave me on my own?" Champ asked.

"You're a man now Champ. Your all that you have! Remember
that once you report to the M.T.C., you are there for 3 months.
No leaving and no visitors. Do what you need to in the 2 day's
you have. Like visit that girl you wanted to."

Champ was anxious to see his angel. He had not seen her
in person for over 2 years. Champ was now 5 inches taller and
60 pounds heavier. What would she think of him now?

Mr. Von pulled in front of the hotel to let Champ off.
Before Champ exited the Lexus jeep Mr. Von spoke. "I know everything
is moving so fast for you Champ. I'm not sure how you are holding
up internally but I'll be available to speak with you whenever
you need me." Mr. Von gave Champ his cell phone number.

"I appreciate it Mr. Von. I feel fine right now." In reality
Champ felt horrible. He did not want to bring up thoughts of
his slain mother. Champ walked stone faced into the hotel lobby
as if nothing in life mattered.

*

The hotel room was ten times larger than where Champ had
spent his previous night. He tossed the items he received from
Mr. Von on the bed farthest from the hotel window. Champ took

a seat on the bed closest to the window. A two bed hotel room.
40 inch T.V.. View from a 4th story window. The parking lot to
the hotel and mall could be seen. Champ let the thoughts come
back. The events of his life ran through his mind. His life was
a horror movie. Somalia would be no better. This all-American
teenager was shitted on by his own Country. The same Country
he was getting ready to put his life on the line for.

   First thing in the morning Champ called Sofia's cell phone
number. She answered on the third ring. "Hello?"

   "Uh hi Sofia. Do you know who this is?"

   "No. Who are you?"

   "It's me Champ!" The excited yelling from the other end
of the line made Champ hold the phone away from his ear.

   "Champ it's you! I can't believe it! Did you get out?
What's going on?" They hadn't spoken in over two years. The juvenile
hall had only allowed for Champ to call his mother.

   "Hey sofia, yes I did get out. I'm in Utah. Provo."

   This was so unexpected for Sofia. She lived in Provo.
As they spoke she was getting ready to go to school. Even though
the now 16 year old Sofia loved Champ, she still had a life to
live while he was locked up. Her 18 year old boyfriend would
be at her house to pick her up in a few minutes.

   "Provo? What? How did you get out here?"

   "I walked!" Champ said jokingly as he thought of what
to tell her. He wanted to tell her the truth but knew Brian was
most likely monitoring every move he made or things he said.

   "No actually I'm out here for my church." Champ fumbled

through the manila envelope to study his cover. Mark Young, Champ
read realizing talking to Sofia was exposing his identity.

"Your church? So you are Mormon? That's great Champ!"

"I want to see you Sofia. Can I take you to lunch after
school?" Champ asked.

"Yeah, I can go to lunch with you."

"Do you still like McDonalds?"

"What, I love it! You remembered?"

"I'll never forget what you like Sofia."

Champ needed to buy some clothes so he went on a shopping
spree with the money Mr. Von gave him. There was a McDonalds
in the mall's parking lot. Sofia's high school was three blocks
away so that's where she walked to meet Champ.

Everything Champ wore was brand-new. Sofia was shocked
at how big Champ had grown in two years. Their hug lasted a full
minute. Sofia did not tell Champ about her current boyfriend.
Sofia was going to spend after school with Josh but told him
she was not feeling well. Champ was Sofia's best friend and she
would lie to many a boyfriend to spend time with him.

They spoke like middle school was just yesterday. Sofia
picked at Champ to figure out what was going on and why he was
in Utah. Champ dropped hint's but quickly changed the course
of conversation. The pair went to see a movie at the mall's movie
theater. After the movie it was getting dark.

"Would you like me to walk you home now?" Champ asked
Sofia as they stood in front of the movie theater.

"No. I don't want to leave you."

"I don't want your folks to worry about you."

"It's okay Champ, they're used to me not coming home." Sofia said with a smile.

"What kind of trouble have you been getting into out here?"

"I don't get in trouble, I just stay at my friends houses sometimes." She didn't mention boyfriend.

"This is good because I have to talk to you."

They went to Champs hotel room but he had Sofia wait for him outside of the door. Champ exited his hotel room with blankets in one hand and a manila envelope in the other.

"Where are we going Champ?" Sofia was having fun. Today with Champ was becoming an adventure for her.

"Follow me Sofia!" Sofia followed Champ to the hotel's fire escape stairs. They were going up. To the roof. The Moon was a big bright in the night sky. Champ laid the blankets down and the two lied on their backs to view the stars.

"It's a shame to be a fish." Champ said.

"Why a fish?" Sofia asked.

"Because they never get to see the beauty of the Moon." They looked at each other and laughed.

"Juvenile hall made you really sweet. But why are you really in Utah, what happened in court?"

"Sofia when you first wrote that you loved me it changed

me. I became humble to life. This may sound corny but I feel
that for you to tell me that you love me, means that I have lived.
My life has been fulfilled!"

Sofia didn't know how to respond. She was extremely flattered
by Champs words. Champ went on to tell Sofia everything. The
surprise visit from the CIA, how they got him out of prison,
the deal he made, his mother, Mr. Von, the M.T.C.. Sofia looked
through the items Mr. Von had given him.

"I lost you once Champ now you're telling me you work for
the CIA and going to Somalia?" Sofia was sad. Champ knew he could
trust Sofia with his life. They shared a superhuman sense of
loyalty to one another.

"Whatever happens I will see you again. Look at me. I
don't know when or how but I will see you again Sofia. Never
forget it!"

They embraced under the warmth of the blankets. It was
the one and only night they would spend together. As they watched
the stars one star looked back at them. Brian knew Champ would
spill the beans to Sofia. She was the only person the kid had.
Brian felt it was good Champ got to vent before he exploded into
a rage of emotions. Brian turned off his access to the Salt Lake
City Trump Card, to give Champ and Sofia privacy.

"I have to thank you for your idea about using this kid.
I think it's going to work out." Brian said to Kim.

"You're the one who made it happen Brian, give yourself
some credit. You did a good job."

"I just don't see how we allowed the kid's mother to be
murdered?" Brian questioned.

"We could have never known she would be killed. What bothers

me is that the T.C. didn't pick it up? It picks up all shooting's
except one involving one of our guy's? That was a first. How
does that happen?"

"Actually Kim it's happened once before." Brian could not
get into details about the first shooting that the T.C. failed
to pick up. The murder of Samuel's wife Lisa was not shared with
the agents at the base.

"What shooting was that?" Kim asked.

"Few years back when T.C. was Red Roomed. I wish I could
fill you in because there appears to be something to this. A
connection to the T.C. not picking up shootings. Maybe a connection
to to a person. I can't put my finger on it yet but I have a
feeling."

"What are you really suggesting Brian?"

"I'm not sure. Call Marty from the San Bernardino FBI
field office and fill him in on the murder of Linda Washington
or Linda Evans. No wait she still went by Washington. Anyway's
see if he can open a case to try and track down her killer. I'm
really interested to see what he can find."

"What if the FBI confirms what you are thinking, will
you start sharing stuff with me?" Kim asked.

"You'll be filled in on everything at that point. You'd
be the only one I could trust with this."

A few day's later Brian looked into the autopsy reports
from Linda and Lisa's murders. The way the bullet entered the
top of both womens skulls was eerily similar. Because Linda's
head exploded the bullets path was traced straight down through
her body to determine it must have entered the top of her skull.
No visable shooter in either shooting. No weapon found connected

to the slaying of Linda, but in Lisa's case a rifle was found and shooter convicted.

Brian had a strong urge to find out what Samuel would have to say if asked questions about the shooting. Brian figured Samuel would get upset and tell him he was wasting the CIA's time on a job that wasn't his. Brian felt more detective than CIA at this point in his career. Desk job's can turn the best physical warrior into the best out of shape thinker.

Brian was ready to get off of his butt. Agent time!

Samuel caught Brian on March's runway before he could board his plane to Washington D.C..

"Brian what's up with this meeting you have with Day?" Oliver Day was the current head of the CIA.

"I'm tired of being shot down for Ghost. I'm going to make my case to him. There is no reason I should be shorted from running this base."

"Brian we have a good thing going here at March. No need to press an issue I delt with already. I have been doing some conferenceing with Day and the President. Day is stepping down next year. Can you guess who the President wants to name as Day's replacement?" Samuel opened his eye's wide as if Brian should have known about his power play.

"You're going to be head? Wow Samuel congratulations!" Brian had no clue.

"Now you can not board that plane and just hold out. When I make my move to Langley, you'll have March. It's yours along with Ghost and every other new toy we have. I'll give you more agents and make sure March becomes the most important base on the West Coast."

"I can't miss my appointment with Day. I have to respect the time he made for me. Don't worry Sam. You'll be painted in nothing but the brightest light."

Samuel smiled waving Brian off. "You stay safe and enjoy your trip!"

It had been two years since Brian had last traveled to the East Coast. He would be staying in Washington D.C.. The City smelled and looked the same. His lung's gave praise for the short break he was giving them from the Inland Empires poor air quality. Brian felt like walking about the city but security deemed it a necessity for a bulletproof Lincoln Town Car to drive him around.

The meeting with Day was brief but impactful. Brian came to learn that his request for access to Ghost was not denied, but never submitted. Why was Samuel lying to him? Why did he want to keep him from using Ghost? Brian would find out in a week when he returned to California. In the meantime he would try to enjoy his week long vacation. The what's, why's would have to be pushed to the back of his mind. Impossible!

Chapter-10


The Missionary Training Center.

    Champ traded juvenile hall for something like a jail.
The differences being the freedoms he had within the M.T.C.,
the education he was receiving, and the fact that he would be
leaving in three months. His thoughts differed. His slain mother.
Thoughts of his night on the roof with Sofia. His possible mission
to Somalia. Somalia! Maybe Somalia would cure the thoughts of
the way his mother was murdered?

    Release Day.

    Champ was sprung from the M.T.C.. Driven by Dr. Von, he
left Utah the same way he came. Champ was flown to a CIA training
facility in Maryland. Learning how to use an A.K.-47 was easy
for Champ. Strategizing and improvising presented more of a challenge
but Champ was able to nail it down within his three months at
the training facility.

Keys. Champ learned this name for the first time. It was what the clan was called. The one he was soon to become a part of.

Brian visited the training facility to see how Champ was doing. Ky, Champs father was set to be released in the summer of 2007. His mothers killer had gotten away with the crime. Champ promised himself he would find the person responsible if he were to survive Somalia.

*

When Brian was on his week long vacation on the East Coast, Samuel was wondering how he could convince his friend that it was better for him not to have knowledge about Ghost. He just would not understand Samuel believed.

Agent Pollard was working Trump Card while Samuel was on the phone with agent Kim Bryant.

"Bryant I need you at base. Your man in The Horn is having some issues but we're busy with an emergency. Get over here A-Sap!"

Kim Bryant had no need for questions. If Samuel was calling on her it was important.

Agent Johnson was speeding down the 215 freeway towards San Diego. A dirty bomb with enough power to level a small city crossed the Mexican border undetected at San Yasidro. The green S.U.V. carrying the device was traveling north on the 15 freeway towards Riverside County. Johnson was speeding towards the S.U.V.. Agent Johnson would head the operation to recover the bomb with the help of twenty Anti-Terrorism officers of the Riverside County Sheriffs Department.

Agent Pollard Ran Trump Card while Samuel directed the situation from behind him. Benson was still on his week long vacation on the East Coast.

"There is an immigration check point on the north bound 15. Have Johnson man the check point and try to remove the driver of the vehicle without incident." Samuel directed.

"Johnson, man the immigration check point on the north bound 15. Take down the driver. T.C. shows no passengers. Dirty bomb confirmed. Backseat, size of a briefcase." Pollard reported to Johnson.

"I copy you. How far out is the package?" Johnson asked.

"Twenty minutes. Johnson you'll have to exit the freeway and get on the north bound lanes or you'll miss the check point and have to double back. That will take too much time!"

"Pollard are you crazy? I don't have sirens! You want me to travel against traffic? That's suicide!"

"We have no other choice if we want to make a stop at the check point. Traffic is light but if we can keep you on the shoulder you can make it safely."

"Where are the C.T.O.'s?"

"They just mobilized out of Riverside. Fifteen minutes from the check point."

"Alright Pollard. Call ahead to I.C.E. and let them know I'm heading their way."

The Immigration Custom and Enforcement agents spotted Johnson's black B.M.W. speeding towards them down the shoulder of the freeway. Sergeant Mazowiecki of I.C.E. burst from his office to meet agent Johnson of the CIA.

"What's the plan?" Sergeant Mazowiecki asked Johnson.

From the base at March agent Pollared called ahead to
Sergeant Mazowiecki and he was told the counter terrorism officers
needed to recover a vehicle driven by a suspected terrorist.

"Just keep running random spot checks. I'll man the lane
our vehicle is in. When I remove the driver hold him until my
team get's here. I'll take the vehicle."

"So you're just asking us to stay out of your way?" Sergeant
Mazowiecki asked with a smug look on his face.

"No, I actually do need your help. As soon as I approach
the vehicle have one of your officers put a cruiser in front
of it." Johnson responded.

"Yeah, I better do that myself. Don't want anybody to
mess it up." Sergeant Mazowiecki said having no faith in his
officers.

Ten minutes passed before two black S.U.V.'s with an Armored
Vehicle approached the check point on the wrong side of the freeway.
Their red and blue lights flashed. The twenty man C.T.O. team
blocked the left lane of the south bound 15.

Johnson ran towards the center divider of the freeway
yelling at his team, "Go Go!" Thrusting his hands forward to
signal he wanted his team to drive off south down the freeway.
"I need you on this side!" The C.T.O.'s drove off needing to
take the ten minute trip for a U-Turn.

Johnson looked at his phone to see where the green S.U.V.
was.

"Shit!" Johnson spit out. The S.U.V. was already here.

"Move!" Johnson yelled at the I.C.E. agent who just waved the green S.U.V. through the check point.

"Stop!" Johnson reached the hood of the S.U.V. before it drove off.

The Caucasian driver looked calm and stared at Johnson with his windows rolled up.

Without speaking Johnson reached to open the drivers door. Locked! Plan B. Johnson cocked his right arm back with a Glock handgun gripped tightly in his fingers. The hand and weapon came forward to smash through the drivers side window.

Sergeant Mazowiecki was having trouble boxing in the S.U.V.. A woman in a purple mini-van was in his way. When the woman moved Sergeant Mazowiecki sped across the lanes to block the S.U.V..

Johnson reached his right arm around the hefty white mans neck, as if he could yank him through the broken window. The.. man floored the gas pedal while bringing a Tech-nine up with his right hand and unloaded a burst! At point-blank range the man fired to the left of Johnson's head. Blowing out his eardrum. Johnson frantically let go and fell to the street.

Sergeant Mazowiecki got the front end of his vehicle in front of the S.U.V. just in time to be spun around and almost flipped. The S.U.V. drifted towards the center divider, crashing into it. The S.U.V. rolled slowly away from the center divider across lanes to it's right.

Johnson jumped to his feet with merely a scratch to his elbow. Johnson looked at the S.U.V. which appeared to be picking up speed north on the 15 freeway. Johnson picked up his Glock and ran to his B.M.W..

Sergeant Mazowiecki joined in on the chase.

The three vehicle's sped north towards the 15-215 interchange. Agent Johnson looked down at his speedometer. 118 MPH! When agent Johnson looked back up the S.U.V. he was chasing was in the air! Quickly hitting his brakes agent Johnson swerved to his right just in time to avoid the concrete freeway divide. Agent Johnson's B.M.W. drifted sideways. The S.U.V. landed on it's roof directly in the path of the drifting B.M.W.. The car slammed into the S.U.V. bringing it to a stop.

Agent Johnson gripped his Glock and ran from his car to the flipped S.U.V.. Gun drawn agent Johnson yelled, "Get out of the vehicle now!"

With no response he crouched low to see there was nobody inside of the S.U.V.. Crawling through a broken back window agent Johnson retrieved the silver briefcase containing the bomb.

When agent Johnson stood from the overturned S.U.V. he put on his Sunglasses and quickly stepped to his car.

"Hey! Where are you going?" Sergeant Mazowiecki yelled towards agent Johnson. Sergeant Mazowiecki stood next to the body of the terrorist who lay deceased in the middle of the freeway.

The C.T.O.'s would arrive to clean up the body. Agent Johnson had to take care of the bomb that now sat in his front passenger seat.

"Pollard I have the weapon. Be at the plane in fifteen minutes!" Standered procedure was to have a plane on standby ready for take off on March's runway. The bomb would then be flown to Peterson Air Force Base in Colorado. Why would today be any different?

"No! Richerdson want's it brought down to the bunker. The planes not ready and the weapon will be safer underground!" Agent Pollard said.

"Copy that Pollard! Hey, I think I need a trip to the hospital after we get the weapon off?" Agent Johnson removed his hand from his left side. There was blood. Agent Johnson got gashed on his left side while climbing through the broken S.U.V.'s window to retrieve the bomb.

As the 215 freeway snaked it's way through Perris agent Johnson looked up at the castle house on the hill. He knew a secret about it that only a person in the CIA would know.

'Where was agent Bryant?' Samuel thought to himself. She won't be here in time! Fuck! Samuel called her phone. "Damn it Kim I said get here! That means thirty minutes ago!"

"Richerdson there is a crash on the 60. The whole freeway is shut down. I have to double back and take Ramona. Problem is C.H.P. is turning traffic around slowly." Agent Bryant was traveling from the direction of her home in Beaumont. The stretch of freeway from Beaumont to Moreno Valley was a dangerous one.

Samuel hung up on Kim and put his phone in his pocket. She would have to be spared. Oh well. At least she was smart. She could still be used. Plus Brian would be devastated if he lost her. Might not recover as a functioning agent?

Agent Johnson exited the elevator with silver briefcase in hand.

"Great job Johnson! Washington will hear all about this!" Samuel said this while giving agent Johnson a high five.

"Ow!" Agent Johnson reached for his side.

"Have a seat, take it easy!" Agent pollard helped agent Johnson to a seat. The briefcase was safely placed on a table in the middle of the bunker.

Samuel looked at his rolex. "I'm going to check on our plane. This is bullshit! I'll be back in five minutes, Stay here!" Samuel entered the elevator to leave this base for the last time. It was becoming a problem for the Agency, in Samuel's mind! The Head didn't want to shut it down, so samuel would take it upon himself. Hire a goon, stage an Iranian terrorist plot on a CIA base. Sacrifice three underperfoming agents, now by luck reduced to two. Brian and Kim would be assigned to another CIA facility in the area to continue working their ongoing missions. Samuel would be moved to D.C. to wait on his promotion.

Samuel sat in his car in the Air Reserve Base parking lot. He pulled his phone from his pocket and dialed the number. The explosion was muted by the bunker.

"Mr. Day there was an explosion at March. We lost two. Pollard. Johnson. Low level." Samuel informed Oliver Day personally of the situation on his cell phone.

"That's a shame Samuel. I'll have to bring you to D.C. soon. Head The Hotel for the time being. Re assign your remaining agents where you see fit."

"I'll assign them to The Hotel with me. Benson's top level and Bryant is a good agent."

"Make sure the clean up is done right! Don't need any slip up's." Oliver Day directed Samuel.

*

The Hotel was an older top secret CIA base built into a hill in the 1970's. In the 1990's it was turned into a CIA prison. It currently held nineteen secret prisoners of the United States. One underground cell block capable of holding two hundred prisoners in secrecy when needed. The Rock Castle that sat directly on top of the hill was over 100 years old.

The city of Perris was growing in all directions around the hill. Under the pretense of a private contractor the CIA was being paid by the city to maintain the area surrounding the Rock Castle, and the structure itself. The Rock Castle was symbolic of Perris historical connection. Nobody but the CIA knew what was going on under The Rock Castle.

Brian and Kim were given brand new equipment to operate Trump Card from The Hotel. Even now that Brian was cleared for Ghost there was no Ghost program for him to use at The Hotel. Without training for Ghost Brian got his questions answered by Samuel.

"It's a weapons program for space. Only used for national security. There is only two Ghost operating stations. One is in D.C. and the other, well it was destroyed at March."

"I see why it's so top secret. What kind of weapon?" Brian asked.

"High power rifle that can hit any target on Earth with one hundred percent accuracy. The Kennedy and King assassinations were close calls for the agency. It took twenty years to come up with Ghost. Remeber Serbian Prime Minister Zoran Djindjic in 2003?"

"Do you ever wonder what side of good we are on Samuel? I know of two recent assassinations right here in our own backyard. Shameful senseless killings of two beautiful women. One of them happened to be your wife!" Brian was enraged that his best friend and future head of the CIA was murdering innocent people.

The normally steeled Samuel was caught off guard by Brian's bluntness. Had it been any other man than the physically gifted

Brian, Samuel would have broke the man's neck in two seconds!
"Despite your quick and flawed judgement my most respected friend,
I will refrain from having you become prisoner number twenty!"
Samuel was angery as he said this.

"If you are the future of the CIA then I don't want any
part of it!"

"Brian you know your accusations changes things between
us?"

"No, Richerdson you changed things when you used the power
of the CIA to murder your wife! And Champs mother? What the hell
was that? Your are a menace! How could Day miss this?"

"Benson your not as important to the agency as you may
think. Day knows how each and every one of his weapons are used.
I would not be taking his place if I murdered my wife!" Oliver
Day did know when and why Ghost was used. He let Samuel handle
his own business. Lord knows Oliver Day was guilty of far worst!

After two weeks at The Hotel Samuel was given an office
in the Pentagon while he waited to replace Oliver Day.

Brian was left in charge of the Intelligence Department
of The Hotel while the prison was run by an agent who played
Warden. Agent Frank Marshall. Marshall had a staff of ten agents
and two nurses to help run the prison.

Agent Ron Davis was informed of the progress of Champ
who was soon to join him in Mogadishu. As of now Ron learned
about deals his clan made with Yemeni pirates to rule the Gulf
of Aden. The only ships off limits were the Chinese. China gladly
supplied the pirates and Somali clan with weapons for safe passage
of it's nations ships.

Ron would be at the Mogadishu airport to give Champ a

warm clan welome! With battles for control of Mogadishu taking place daily Champ was sure to be in the middle of the violence from the start. Sacrificing himself for a country that didn't even love him.

Chapter-11

January 2006.

Champ was flown to the United Arab Emirates. Once in the U.A.E. Champ boarded an Air Somalia flight from Sharjah to Mogadishu.

The plane landed. Champ exited the plane. At the bottom of the stairs was Ron with seven clan members. Ron's cover name; Ahmed Adan. General Ahmed Adan! Champs name; Abdi Daar.

Abdi (Champ) was born in Somalia. His parents snuck illegally into the United States through Mexico. Never a citizen of the U.S. Abdi was discovered after the murder of his parents in Los Angeles. General Ahmed (Ron) was Abdi's uncle. Thus he welcomed him back home. This was the cover. Nobody from the clan would know they were CIA.

Ron with all other clan members had an AK-47 slung over his shoulder. The way an American need's a cell phone is equal to a clan member needing his AK! Mogadishu was a war zone with clan and government constantly struggling to control it.

"Abdi my boy! I'm so happy to have you back!" The 24 year old General hugged Champ.

"Me as well! I missed you!" Champ replied. It was humid in Mogadishu. Champ was nervous with all of the guns around him. He would get used to it.

"This is the American gangster?" Kimbo looked at the General with skepticism. "You are Crip, Blood?" The 6'5 250 pound Kimbo asked Abdi.

"No, I'm from South Central, but I'm not a Crip or a Blood." Champ responded.

"Let's get to the hut!" The general ordered. The men filled the two cars. Champ sat next to Kimbo in the backseat of the black Toyota Corola. Stick drove with Ron in the front passenger seat. Eye's wide open so they wouldn't end up in a casket with their eye's wide open.

Leaving the Airports gate's the few newer high rises in the city made the older buildings look worse than they actually were. The Potal (as this street was locally known) ran Northeast from the airport to the edge of the city. The street passed through four areas of the city controlled by four different groups. Al-Shabaab had control of sixty percent of the city. Hizbul Islam had twenty percent while the Transitional Federal Government (TFG) had ten percent.

Ron led the surge against the TFG which gained the Kismayo East Youth, or better known as Keys ten percent of the city. The Keys named their area of the city The Hut.

The Hut consisted of various four story housing buildings surrounded by a shopping district, and four neighborhoods of single story housing. Directly in-between the TFG and Hizbul Islam territories.

Originating in South Somalia's Jubbada Hoose the Keys and Al-Shabaab were in a war for control of the entire South. Al-Shabaab was stronger with more momentum than the countries forty-eight clans with struggling Government put together.

Champ stared out of the car window. The armed men lounging in the city streets contradicted the war they were in the middle of. They looked relaxed.

"Your Uncle is very important Abdi. Our General." Kimbo said this with a bright smile. Kimbo smoked a cigar, "That's what makes you important Abdi! As General Ahmed's nephew you are one of us, a Key!"

Key? Champ studied his mission thoroughly. He read about what the Keys were; a large clan started in the city of Kismayo. Fishermens sons in the Eastern portion of Kismayo became wealthy Pirates. Led by the youthful leader Aar Ali, the gang grew into a clan. Aar Ali became a warlord. His nickname of Double-A changed to Da Da. Da Da made a deal with the Chinese to spare the Chinese cargo ships from piracy. In return the Chinese supplied the Keys with weapons. Da Da led a war against Al-Shabaab taking control of Kismayo and half of southern Somalia.

The fight for Mogadishu was a hard one. Da Da put Ron in charge of taking the strategic city for the Keys. Ron started as a Pirate, then fought hard for Da Da against Al-Shabaab and the Ethiopians. Many in the clan believed if Ron could win control of Mogadishu he was sure to be next in line for leader of the Keys.

"Key? What is a Key?" Champ asked Kimbo but already knew the answer.

"Shit Key! You are my Key now Abdi! We're a big family. Stick is your Key! The Keys behind us are your Keys! The Hut is all Key! Soon the whole city will be Key! Somalia is ours. We just have to get rid of the trash first. You're from America so I don't know if you are ready for this real African shit? Somalia Key! We get it Crackin!"

"I've seen violence my whole life. Been shot. I'm ready to die anyway!" Champ said to Kimbo.

"I like you already Abdi! I'm Kimbo. If you have any problems or need anything call on Kimbo. I got you my Key!"

"I'll remeber that Kimbo."

"You need a name Abdi, how about Wal-Mart?" Kimbo laughed at his American joke.

"Don't let Kimbo call you Wal-Mart Abdi! That shit will stick once we get to the hut." Ron advised Champ.

"Yeah Kimbo, I don't want to be known as Wal-Mart." Champ said.

"Alright Key, I will call you Cali! You come from Cali right? That's gangster American right?"

"Yeah Key I'm cool with that!" Champ answered.

The two Toyota Corolas pulled into a dead end street in The Hut called the West End. Two-hundred Keys were out in full force to welcome the new important Key. The Generals nephew. From America! The Sun was bright. The General and Champ exited the same side of the vehicle. Twenty-five trucks fitted with anti-aircraft, anti-tank, and heavy machine guns formed a large perimeter around the group of hundreds.

Champ was taken aback when he saw how quiet the large crowd was. Ron spoke to them.

"This is my nephew Abdi from America. Treat him with the same respect as you would treat me. Kimbo has named him Cali and that is what our new Key will be known by. Stay alert and on point! The TFG may be targeting the shopping district tonight. They have night-vision goggles that make them see in the dark. I have five such goggles. I'll give them out tonight but don't forget! When you kill a TFG soldier take his goggles. Da Da is with us my Keys!" Da Da was worshiped by the Keys. In reality Da Da now spent most of his time in Dubai put up in an expensive condo.

The Key called Trouble approached Champ and shook his hand, "What's up my Key!"

Champ felt warmth from the Keys. Like a family. He was being accepted by one of the largest clans in Somalia. The feeling of belonging to the most lethal and powerful clan in the World (the CIA) was becoming faint. Champ now known as Cali would rather be a Key. It felt right. Like he was amongst brothers. Regardless of his own feelings Champ would have to remain loyal to his Country as well as the CIA. The CIA ran the World. Even within the Keys the CIA held power. A powerful General in Ron and a new foot soldier in Champ.

"So you are the kid they sent me?" Ron spoke to Champ. the two stood alone with the birds on the roof of the four story building. Ron's command post and residence.

"I'm honored to meet you General Ahmed." Champ spoke knowing not to use each others names.

Metal barriers lined the roof of the building seven feet high to serve as protection from snipers. "Abdi how'd they get you?"

"Freedom, money. How did you get into this?" Champ asked.

"Little bit of craziness on my part. After a tour in Iraq I couldn't deal with life in the States. The angency brought this up and I jumped on it." Ron replied.

"What should I expect?" Champ asked.

"The unexpectable! You're Cali now. Member of the Keys. Nephew of me, the General."

"How often do we talk to base?"

"Once a month if nothing important is going on. I'll call now." Ron pulled out his cell phone and dialed the angency number that would be routed through a building in San Francisco. Anybody trying to eavesdrop on the conversation would hear only static.

Ron put the cell phone to his ear. Champ looked around the roof. The Sun was going down. Champ looked through a gun slot in one of the metal barriers. A street in front of the building was still filled with Keys. A school was across the street. This street dead ended to a brick wall. On the other side of the wall was The Huts shopping district. Always busy the keys policed the area. A large hole in the wall provided for easy access from the West End to the shopping district.

"Kim this is Ahmed. I received Abdi, it's a touchdown." Ron spoke into his cell phone.

"Good Ron. How is he taking to it?"

Ron glanced at the kid looking through the gun hole, "Pretty good I would say. He was already given a name."

"What's that?"

"Cali."

"Interesting choice."

"Is Benson there?"

"No. He has been busy lately but I will be here for you."

"Do you want to speak with the kid?"

"Yeah, put him on."

"Cali!" Ron summoned him over to get the phone.

"Never knew so much hell could loom under such a beautiful day." Champ said while walking towards Ron to get the cell phone. Many men with guns could be seen clearly from Champs vantage point.

"Just wait until the night. It's like the fourth of July." After handing Champ the phone Ron went to enter the building, "When you are done come down, we have a meeting."

Champ nodded his head at Ron.

"Hello!" Champ spoke into the cell phone.

"Hey Champ how are you getting along?" Kim asked.

"I'm okay so far. Is this Kim?"

"Yes, I am Kim. Ron should be giving you a cell phone with a direct link to base. I will be here to help you when needed. Ron will explain your mission as things move along."

"Is Brian there?"

"No but I'll inform him you would like to speak."

"I better go inside. Ahmed said there's a meeting downstairs."

"Stay alert Champ." Kim wished him well knowing there was a high chance of death in Champs future.

When Champ entered the meeting area (General Ahmed's living room) Ron sat at the head of a long table. Marijuana and Tobacco smoke filled the room. Champs system was not well ajusted. The fifteen seats at the table were filled. One seat taken by Ron and fourteen taken by his underlings. The finest, smartest fourteen fighters of the Keys. All between the ages of seventeen through twenty-four. Young killers at the apex of their short life expectancy. Champ stood in one corner of the room while the men spoke.

"If we just let the TFG stroll into the district without a fight they could get the upper hand. We could lose hold of it." Yusuf a yellow skinned twenty year old spoke up.

"He's right General. We should fight them off from ever entering. Block the streets with our trucks, and man the roofs." The obese twenty-four year old spoke. The food aide from the U.S. fed him well.

"We thought of that already." Trouble spoke, "They'll just send waves from two different directions. Once they blow passed one barricade they will have control. Lull um to sleep, that's how we have to do it. Let them feel comfortable like we left. They trap themselves. We lay them down."

Ron stood up and received a bag from one of his wives. The General had five wives. Three in Kismayo and two with him here in Mogadishu. He placed the bag on the table, then pulled out a pair of night vision goggles. "Cali come here. You get a pair of these. It's your first mission as a Key and I don't want you killed on your first day. You will be with Trouble on the roofs."

Champ was stone faced trying to mask his nervousness when his new moniker was spoken. Trouble noticed Champ was uncomfortable. Trouble quickly stood, grabbed the goggles and walked them to Champ who stood in the background of the room in a dark corner. Trouble smiled and passed Champ the goggles.

"Come on Key, need to get you hooked up!" Champ followed Trouble to a different room in the building. Trouble did three quick knocks on the door with a slap to let the Keys in the room know it was him. A 16 year old boy named Dirt opened the door, "What's cracking Key?" Dirt spoke.

"Homeboy it smells like that California sunshine in this mothafucka." Trouble referred to the chronic smoke in the room. They entered the room. Dirt looked at Champ.

"What's up Key my name is Dirt!" He extended his hand.

"I'm Cali!" Champ shook his hand. In the room was a crew of sixteen Keys. All teenagers led by the Twenty-one year old Trouble. This tight group of Keys were like brothers. They grew up together, fought together, and had no problem dying for one another.

"What's up Key!" Hussein got off of a worn couch across from a 16" T.V., whith Desert Eagle in hand he approached Champ. "Are you ready to die?" The question was blunt.

Champ did not want to die but knew never to show he feared it, "Only as a man!" Champ responded.

"My Key I like that. You need a gun to survive out here. Without one your are a victim." Hussein said.

"Omar!" Trouble called out to the 16 year old loading

a clip at a table. "Go with Hussein to get Cali heated!"

Omar with Hussein took Champ to the Keys armory. This
room was filled with enough weapons and ammo to make a U.S. Army
Battalion happy.

"It's all here Key. Whatever you are comfortable with.
Me? I just stick with my AK. Easy to use, clean, and it's deadly!"
Hussein said to Champ. They stood in front of everything from
a small twenty-two handgun to grenade-launchers.

"What's that?" Champ was looking towards a gun that reminded
him of Kobe Bryant's Black Mamba Symbol.

"Oh yeah, yeah, that's the one we call Oh Fuck!" Hussein
said this after which he and Omar burst into laughter.

Champ laughed too but did not know what was so funny.
"Why do you call it Oh Fuck?" Champ asked.

Hussein told Champ with a smile, "We got it from a Ukrainian
ship. I climbed on board the ship with Kimbo, and a crewman had
it mounted on the deck. The first thing we said when we saw it
pointed at us was Oh Fuck!" Hussein and Omar burst into laughter
again.

"What happened to the grewman who pointed the gun at you?"
Champ asked wondering why they were not killed by Oh Fuck.

"He never fired. Just pointed. Kimbo shot him." Hussein
said.

What the Keys called Oh Fuck was really three AK-47's
welded to the back of one another. The three AK's spun firing
like a gattling gun.

"I'm going to call it the Black Mamba." Champ told hussein

and Omar as he approached to pick up the weapon.

Omar gave Hussein a look of, is this Key serious? Champ was very serious.

"Naw Key it's too heavy and you have to mount it everytime you use it." Omar approached Champ to try and talk him into another weapon.

It was too late. Champ fell in love with the weapon at first sight. Omar and Hussein were both surprised at how easy Champ lifted the weapon to his shoulder. The image was menacing.

"We'll be on the roofs tonight. This will be perfect for me." Champ said.

"The roofs?" Hussein questioned.

"Yeah that's where my uncle wants us, I was at the meeting."

"That's cool with me Key! Hussein we got Generals Ahmed's nephew on the squad now, we will always get the easy work!" Omar said happily.

"The roofs aren't any easier than the street. It's all the same to me." Hussein responded.

Champ also grabbed an Uzi stuffing it into his waistband. He was ready for war. Before returning to Troubles war room, Hussein filled a bag with a handful of Marijuana, "Get some Key!" Hussein said to Champ.

The Keys kept bricks of Marijuana for it's fighters.

"I don't smoke." Champ responded.

"You will after tonight Key!" Omar assured him.

Had these kid's been on another continent they would be getting ready for school the next day. Not in the Horn of Africa. Not in Somalia. At least not yet. If Ron Davis (Known to Africa as General Ahmed Adan) continued to have it his way he would turn the Keys into friends of the United States. Being friends with the United States would help build the countries infrastructure. Eventually the Keys would be Somalia's government. Ron kept his American ideals to himself at the moment.

Da Da the still reigning leader of the Keys was strengthening the Keys relationship with the Chinese. The Keys only did business with China and Yemen. China knew if the Keys took the entire country they would have access to all of Somalia's resources. Uranium, Natural Gas, Oil. Not to mention the strategic importence for China's growing military.

Ron had plans to turn the TFG's offensive into their biggest mistake. After smashing them in the shopping district, like a boxer countering a jab the TFG will be exposed for an attack.

Trouble now had everybody in his war room strapped up and ready to go. They would rain down hell upon the TFG until there was no more resistance. Upon Troubles orders the Keys will mass in the street until Ron gave the orders to push the TFG out of Mogadishu. Gaining more territory within the city would only help bolster the Keys credibility with the people, while sending it's rival clan's a stern warning; the Keys are strong and here to stay!

Chapter-12


It was night. Champ had his Uzi in one hand. Duffle bag
with the Black Mamba and night vision goggles in the other. All
eighteen members of Trouble's crew were walking to the shopping
district. They would climb to the roof of the laundry cleaners
building.

An eight year old boy in The Hut approached Champ. The
boy didn't have a shirt or shoes. His ribs were all he was. Walking
bones. The poor boy was starving.

"Can you bring me back food?" The boy asked Champ.

Trouble tried to keep Champ moving. Champ stopped to talk
to the boy. He saw himself in the boy's eye's. "What's your name?"
Champ asked.

"Bile." The boy replied.

Champ put the duffle bag down. Still holding the Uzi as

if it was glued to his hand, Champ pulled a candy bar from the bag handing it to Bile.

"What's this?" Bile asked never before seeing a snickers bar.

Champ opened the wrapper and handed it back to Bile, "Eat it, you'll like it!" Champ assured the boy.

"He can't eat that Cali! It will make him sick." Trouble said while reaching to take the candy bar from the boy.

"No!" The boy yelled. Bile ran with the candy bar to a group of similar starving children.

'No wonder why so many kid's join clans,' Champ thought to himself. All of the Keys ate well. Before leaving for the shopping district Champ ate a big bowl of rice and beans. Ron fed his fighters first, then he let a small percentage of the Keys food go to the community. Bile and his family were one of the many who didn't receive any food from the Keys.

Champ looked back at Bile before walking through the hole in the wall that led to the shopping district. Bile gave the candy bar to his two little sisters with out getting any for himself. Bile would go hungry so that his sisters could eat.

All was quiet on the roofs. The Keys laid low as to not be seen. Champ wore the night vision goggles. He had the Black Mamba next to him on stand-by.

"They're coming!" Champ told Trouble who was crouched next to him.

The TFG rolled into the main street of the shopping district. Large trucks carrying TFG soldiers drove cautiously. TFG soldiers on foot jogged alongside the trucks. A total of fifteen TFG trucks

came to a stop within the shopping district. The TFG assumed
the Keys must have abandoned the district.

Big Boy's group of Keys was the first to get off. Just
as the TFG soldiers began exiting the large trucks a rocket was
fired at the last and first truck to pull into the district.
The TFG were now officially trapped in a shooting range being
shot at from all sides. No wonder why they were losing the war.
The Keys heavy caliber weapons mounted on trucks were driven
to block off both ends of the street.

Champ had the Black Mamba mounted on the side of the roof.
He fired the triple barreled AK47 gattling gun at the street.
Champ missed on purpose. Trouble spotting Champs horrible aim,
took control of the Black Mamba.

With deadly accuracy Trouble ripped apart twelve TFG soldiers.
Champ watched murder in sickness. He hated it but it was a requirement
to be cold hearted in this mission.

Champ took aim down upon a TFG soldier hiding behind a
car. He aimed at the mans legs and fired a few rounds. The man
drug his body under the car after being shot in the leg.

With all of the gun fire it was hard to hear. "Get down!"
was faintly heard on the roof. Champ looked around just in time
to see another roof manned by the Keys had become compromised.
A TFG soldier stood on the roof and fired a shoulder mounted
rocket at the Keys.

Champ dove for his life. The rocket exploded in the center
of the roof killing Omar and four other Keys.

The heat of the explosion burnt Champs fingers as he held
onto the side of the building. He had to let go! Champ fell in
the alley, trash softened his fifteen foot fall. It was dark.
The gun fire was loud on all sides. Champ could see the hole

in the wall that led to the west end. Champ lost the night vision
goggles but the Uzi managed to stay in his waistband. The hole
in the wall was one hundred feet ahead of him.

Making sure the Uzi was ready to fire Champ sprinted.
Behind Champ was murderous carnage. In front of him the west
end appeared deserted. Champ knew the Keys had snipers on point.
He may be mistaken for a TFG soldier and shot if he wasn't cautious.
Champ stuck to the shadows trying to get back to General Ahmed's
building. Looking back over his Shoulder while approaching the
door to Ahmed's building brought Champ a surprise when he righted
his head. A dark hooded figure stood in front of him. AK47 pointed
in his face caused his heart to palpitate. His eye twitched.
Palms sweated.

"I'm Key! I'm cool, don't shoot me!" Champ Pleaded.

"If you are Key why aren't you in the district?" The war
could be heard raging on in the distance.

"I was with Trouble but the TFG hit us with a rocket.
I'm General Ahmed's nephew Cali. This is the only place I knew
to come."

The AK was lowered. The voice of the  dark hooded figure
grew femininely friendly. "Get in here Cali!" They entered the
building. The hood was now down. Champs heart continuted to palpitate.
Not from fear but because of how gorgeous this Nubian Queen was.
With face and body of Alicia Keys Champ wished she could be his
superwoman.

"Cali I'm Malia. I saw you in the meeting earlier." Malia
smiled at Champ.

His voice stuttered to life, "Malia! That's a beautiful
name. You are beautiful!"

Malia was flattered, "Come on, let's go upstairs. You look shot out."

That was an understatement, Champ was exhausted. Malia led him up the stairs. He watched her figure with every step she took.

"Here you go," Malia opened the rooms door. "You can sleep on the couch."

Champ looked around the room. It looked familure. "This is my uncles room!" Champ looked to Malia.

She smiled, "It's my room too. I'm his wife."

Champ thought to himself, 'not only did I run away from the battle today, but now I'm alone with the Generals wife! This is not good'. Too stressed over what tomorrow would bring Champ laid on the couch and was fast to sleep.

*

The war raged on! Standing in the middle of street after street, Champ was watching the ground turn red around him. TFG slodiers were pushed out of the city to Jawhar. The Keys fought long hard day's and night's against the two remaining clans in the city. Champs bond with Trouble grew battle by battle. Trouble's group of Keys now numbered eight. Trouble himself, Champ, Hussein, Dirt, the twins Haji and Mahdi, Bantu, amd Dark Side.

Sixteen months after Champ arrived in Somalia the city of Mogadishu fell to the Keys. It was not easy and the young Champ felt as if fighting for the Keys had taken his soul! Three people! That was the number of people Champ felt he had killed. The men were trying to kill him but still. They were human beings!

Maybe a little crazed but still. His brothers.

After many battles Trouble noticed that Champ appeared
to feel compassion for the men they were fighting. Instead of
chest wounds, Champ always aimed for the enemies leg's. Through
all of his wars Trouble never had a fighter like Champ. He thought
before he shot.

It had now been over a year since the young Champ arrived
in Mogadishu. In the spring of 2007 Champ was 18 years old. The
city of Mogadishu was war-torn and freshly won by the Keys.

Ron was the undisputed Governor. Only having Da Da to
answer to he held close to absolute power. The area surrounding
Mogadishu was loosely patrolled by the Keys. During one of these
patrols Ron was called and informed of a large group of people
walking towards Mogadishu. They were walking from the direction
of Afgooye. A small city still controlled by Al-Shabaab to the
west of Mogadishu.

Trouble's group of Keys was sent to investigate. Anybody
coming from Afgooye was suspect. Trouble got in the back of a
white Toyota truck next to Mahdi who manned the 50 Calibar Machine
Gun mounted in the bed of the truck. Mahdi's twin brother Haji
drove the truck with Dirt in the passenger seat.

Champ climbed into the back of a similar truck with Dark
Side manning the 50 Cal. Hussein drove this truck with Bantu
taking the passenger seat. Bantu put 50-Cents Get Rich Or Die
Trying in the C.D. player. 50-Cent was a favorite of the clan.

Champ was only 18 years old but now an expert of Somali
clan warfare. The CIA could only gather intelligence on the political
situation within Somalia when what they really needed to know
was what China was using the Keys for? With shadow war no favor
went unrewarded. With Ron and Champ in Mogadishu the angency
was missing out on the things taking place in Kismaayo. Ron was

working on getting Da Da to let Kimbo take control of Mogadishu
so he could return to Kismaayo. As of now Da Da wanted his best
in charge of holding on to the capital city. Ron was stuck for
now but he was going to send Champ along with Trouble and his
crew to Kismaayo.

Champ stood in the back of the truck as they sped down
the wide unpaved road towards Afgooye. He saw them in the dusty
distance. Walking along the side of the road to his left. It
was a group of thirty people. Women and children. Appearing to
be refugees from al-Shabaab.

Champ felt a sigh of relief when he realized they were
only refugees. He wouldn't have to kill anybody today. The two
Key trucks came to a stop next to the refugees.

"Hello! Where are you coming from?" Trouble asked the
group while maintaining his position in the back of the truck.

"Afgooye!" A elder gray hair woman spoke for the group,
"al-Shabaab, they took our homes, food, water. We have nothing!"

Trouble was just about to order his Keys to get the refugees
water when a thought crossed his mind. How did a refugee from
Afgooye know he wasn't al-Shabaab?

"Where are you headed?" Trouble asked the woman who was
walking up to the truck.

"You are Key right?" Trouble didn't get a chance to answer
and he wasn't going to. Trouble turned to look at Champ just
as the woman detonated her suicide vest! Trouble felt bad for
not only leading the Keys into an ambush, but for the young Champ
who would not fight women and childrn. Troubles Keys were doomed!

The explosion lifted the truck on it's side. Haji lay
dead on top of Dirt who was trapped in the cabin of the truck.

Trouble and Mahdi were thrown onto the side of the unpaved road. Mahdi remained conscious while Trouble lay unconscious bleeding from the side of his face and skull.

Hussein put his truck in reverse at the sight of the explosion. Champ dropped to the bed of the truck. AK47 bullets tore into the truck. Dark Side had no choice in the land of kill or be killed. He opened up the 50-Caliber on the group. Women and children with smoking AK's hit the ground. With luck for them Hussein caught a round to his face causing the truck to swerve and flip over. Dark Side was flung, Champ was under the bed of the truck.

Mahdi was chopped down almost as soon as he stood. These Keys were in jeopardy of being taken as prisoners of al-shabaab. Champ rolled out from under the flipped truck just to be met by AK's pointed in his direction. Champ quickly raised his hands to signal his surrender.

Champ, Dirt, Dark Side, Bantu, and Trouble were rounded up and forced to sit in the middle of the road. The other three Keys were dead. The survivng Keys were on their knees made to face down, except trouble. He was hurt from the blast and laid on his side.

Trouble spoke to Champ through clinched teeth, "I should have saw this coming. Al-Shabaab used it against the TFG for years. Send out refugees to capture prisoners."

"Are they going to kill us?" Champ asked.

"They'll try to use us first. Don't let them know who you are. They will treat you worse and ask for more from General Ahmed."

Champ looked up to see a bus approaching from the direction of Afgooye. Black hoods were placed over their heads. Al-Shabaab was coming for them.

\*

Like a father watching his son be kidnapped  Brian Benson
called Ron and demanded he send Keys to rescue Champ from the
road before he was taken to Afgooye.

"It was a set up Ron! Al-Shabaab has them in a bus, they're
driving them back towards Afgooye!" Brian yelled into the phone.

Ron turned his phone off. "Kimbo! Time to move on Afgooye!"

"General I thought we were going to wait?" Kimbo asked
confused.

"Shabaab got my nephew and Trouble out side of the city.
Set us up! Call Big Boy and get the Keys ready. We're taking
all we have." Ron put on his vest, loaded his two glocks and
holster them. It was he who was responsible. Out smarted by al-
Shabaab. Ron needed to spill blood to get his Keys back. No negotiatian!

The tanks, trucks, and helicopters of the Keys were leaving
Mogadishu with a thunderous roar. Ron led his Keys towards Afgooye
down the same road Champ was taken from. The Keys drove passed
the two destroyed trucks. They had already been stripped of their
50-Caliber Machine Gun's. The three dead Keys were loaded onto
the back of a truck that took their bodies back to Mogadishu.
They would be given a true Key style funeral. Float the bodies
to sea just like Da Da did the first Key casualty of war in Kismaayo.

\*

The Keys taken by al-Shabaab were locked in a large empty
freezer. The freezer did not work but served as an adequate makeshift
jail cell. The hoods were removed from over their heads.

"Trouble wake up my Key!" Champ took off his shirt. After ripping it Bantu helped tie it around the bleeding wound on Trouble's skull. Trouble suffered a concusiòn. He still lay unconscious.

"I don't know how much longer he has!" Bantu spoke to Champ. Dirt and Dark Side sat against one wall of the freezer contemplating how the enemy was going to kill them.

"We have to wake him up. If he stay's asleep he will fall into a coma and die." Champ said.

"Wake up! Trouble, wake up my Key!" Bantu said while peeling Trouble's eyelid back.

"I got an idea," Champ said, "Hold his arms Bantu."

"Why hold his arm Cali?"

"To keep him from hitting me if he wakes up!" Champ responded.

Champ slid his fingers under the shirt into the wound on Trouble's skull and squeezed.

"Owww!" Trouble awoke, "What the fuck happened? Bantu let me go!"

Bantu let go of Trouble and he stood up.

"Relax Trouble! You had a concusion, we had to wake you up." Champ tried to calm his Key.

Trouble looked around the freezer, "Where are we, what happened Cali?"

"You don't remember? We drove into an ambush. Haji, Mahdi, and Hussein were killed. Al-Shabaab brought us to this freezer and locked us in." The door to the freezer opened as Champ finished his sentence.

"You!" A high ranking member of al-Shabaab was looking at Champ. The man was surrounded by men in all black and ski mask. "Come with us!" The man spoke.

Champ was led out of the freezer which was re-locked shut. They exited an abandoned gas station which was bieng guarded by two kid's with AK's who looked too young to be teenagers.

Champ was forced to sit in the backseat of a black car with tinted windows, next to the high ranking al-Shabaab member. A masked gunman sat twisted in his front passenger seat with his weapon trained on Champ. One wrong move and Champs blood would make a mess of the man next to him. The car pulled away from the gas station and drove off through the streets of Afgooye. Champ had never traveled out side of the Capitol city of Somalia. He had no clue where he was.

"Do you know who I am?" The high ranking man asked Champ with a deep voice, while staring at him.

"No, but I respect you." Champ didn't know why he said that. Just wanted to appease the man.

"You respect me but you don't know who I am?" The man gave a hefty laugh, "I know who you are. We have been watching you." The man pulled out pictures of Champ with Ron in Mogadishu.

Champ looked at the pictures then asked, "What do you need with me?"

"Awe that's a good question Cali! You'll find out when we get to Addis Ababa."

Champs stomic turned inside out which caused him to puke in the mans car. Addis Ababa is the capital city of Ethiopia.

Maybe this wasn't al-Shabaab who had captured him? Regardless of what was true the butt stock from an AK to Champs chin was and he was knocked unconscious.

\*

When Ron rolled into Afgooye with his Keys the city was deserted of al-Sahbaab soldiers. The only fire fight was between two outgunned kid's in front of a gas station. They thought it was smart to fire at the first wave of Keys to enter the city. The Keys quickly knocked them down.

Ron went to the gas station as soon as he was notified a group of Keys were found alive inside of a freezer.

"Trouble where's my nephew?" Was Ron's first question without mind to Trouble's bad condition.

"They took him General Ahmmed, left us to die!" Trouble said while being held up by two other Keys.

"Why in the fuck would they take him? What did you tell them?" The General demanded an immediate answer.

"They never even spoke to us. A man came, called Cali out and left us here General." Bantu spoke up.

"Put them in a truck and get them back to the city!" Ron ordered. He was mad that he lost Champ. He waited over three years for the CIA to send him help. A year into having a partner he lost him to the enemy. He had to call Brian Benson and give him the news. From the roof at his compound in Mogadishu Ron called Brian. "I messed up Brian. The day before I was going to send him to Kismaayo I got the kid killed!"

"Don't be so sure he's dead Ron! I tracked al-Shabaab crossing the border at Dolo Odo into Ethiopia." Brian said from his operation center at The Hotel. Brian now had three agents assigned to him to run Trump Card and also assist in his Somali mission. This was the first time in the history of the angency that an undercover agent held so much power in a terrorist group.

"Ethiopia? How is that possible Brian? The Ethiopians would never let al-Shabaab cross their border."

"I know Ron. We might have to send SEAL's out on this one? After we get him back we can leave him in a house in Afgooye for one of your Keys to find him?"

"You can get him out of Ethiopia without blowing our cover?" Ron Asked.

"My former partner is running things in Langley now. I have some pull." Brian was referring to Samuel Richerdson who was now the head of the CIA. Literally influencing the World from a chair in Langley Virginia.

"Let me know what you find out about this new Ethiopian connection. I'll work on Da Da letting me go back to Kismaayo." Ron said.

"Stay safe Ron! I'll let you know when we get Champ back to Afgooye."

Brian hung up his phone and turned to agent Kim Bryant, "I'll have to call in a favor from Sam."

Kim looked surprised. "What happened to", Kim changed her voice to mock Brian, "I'll never talk to that scumbag again until I get him to step down?"

Brian smirked and told Kim, "I have to get Champ out of

Ethiopia and Sam's the only person I know who can get that done. I will get back to hating the man later." Brian dialed Samuel's number.

Chapter-13


        The summer of 2007 Ky Washington was 45 years old.
Just three months before this day Ky was called into the counselors
office and told he would be released parole free! The grown man
cried in his wheelchair. Since becoming paralyzed from the waist
down Ky lived closer to his Koran than ever before. Ky let hate
escape his body. What he once thought as a white mans world,
was now the rich mans world. Ky didn't hate the rich. Just acknowledged
they ran the world. Ky took his surprise release date as a gift
from Allah. He didn't know his son sold himself to the government
in exchange for their freedom. All he knew was that in 2006 his
ex-wife and son stopped writing to him. No explanation. Like
he didn't exsist. Call's to Linda's phone went unaccepted for
a month until the line was disconnected.

        Outlaw was Ky's cellmate. He jumped down off of the top
bunk to wish Ky well, "My brother don't forget to stay humble
out there. Temptation will be many. Never forget how many of
us never get out!" Outlaw said to Ky.

"I sit in a wheelchair. I'm reminded everyday to stay humble. I'm on a mission to find my son. All I have is this envelope with my ex-wifes address on it. They moved to Perris. It's been a year since I last heard from them. My son was facing life in prison. I'm worried about what might have happened." Ky said.

"I'm sure things turned out alright, stay positive! That's where your going, perris? Where is that at, Orange County?"

"No. It's in Riverside. The Inland Empire."

"That's the I.E., it has to be better than L.A.?"

"Yeah, it's cool." The door to the cell opened.

"Washington get you stuff, you're being released!" Was said over the intercom in the dayroom.

Ky left his property to his celli. All he took was his ex-wifes and Champs letters. He couldn't wait to see them. Ky wore gray sweats and a pair of black and white hi-top Nike basketball shoes for release clothes.

Ky and his wheelchair were helped into a white van. He was driven by a correctional officer from Crescent City (the home of Pelican Bay State Prison) to Santa Rosa. At the Amtrack Station Ky road the train to Union Station in downtown Los Angeles.

Union Station was busy in the afternoon. Ky was uncomfortable in public after spending ten years in prison. Ky rolled the back of his wheelchair to a wall. He bumped a well dressed white woman talking on a cell phone. She jumped away, "Oh my God sir you scared me!" The woman placed her hand over her heart. She smiled at Ky then went back to talking on her cell phone.

"I'm sorry, I'm sorry!" Ky said to the woman who clearly ignored him as she was deep back into her phone conversation.

Ky closed his eye's and his thoughts drifted back to 1996.
To the front of their home on 60th Street Ky threw the baseball
to his 7 year old son Champ.

Champ wore his fathers Dodgers hat. Champ took the ball
out of his glove. He wound up to throw, "That's right Champ.
Give me a fastball!" His father cheered him on, "It's all in
the wind up." Ky advised his son.

Champ gave a confidant look to his father. With the poise
of the Los Angeles Dodgers pitcher Hideo Nomo, Champ pitched
the ball to his father as fast as he could throw it. More of
a Ferdinand Magellan the ball sailed clearly around his father
like Magellian's expedition's around the world.

Ky smiled at his son, "You'll get it soon enough. Come
on let's go inside! Mom should have lunch for us!" When Ky looked
at the front door the Goddess herself was standing there watching
her boy's.

"You're right, I do have lunch! Who want's turkey sandwiches?"
Linda asked gracefully.

Ky caught Champ trying to out run him for the door. Ky
lifted his son to his shoulders, "Ah little man you are going
to have to move faster than that if you want to be a Dodger!
Hold on tight!" Ky leaned forward through the doorway with Champ
hanging on tightly to him. Linda's warm hand was on his arm.
So much love! Her hand was so warm!

Ky was snapped back to reality by the screeches of a train
coming to a stop. "Hey buddy! Buddy!" Ky opened his eye's to
see a security official tapping the side of his wheelchair with
a baton. "You can't be loitering here, board a train or leave
sir." The stern looking caucasian man ordered Ky rudely.

Ky looked at the man and thought of what Ice Cube said

on a West Side Connection song; 'I feel institutionalized, and I'm on the street's.'

"Did you hear me?" The man demanded, "Go back to skid row, you can't loiter here!"

Ky didn't get mad at the mans blatant ignorance. Instead he smiled at the man and said, "I'm sorry sir. I'll just go buy my ticket now." Ky rolled away from the man.

"You do that!" The man said to the back of Ky's wheelchair.

Ky didn't hear him. He just as soon forgot the man existed. Ky held Linda's letter in his hands and looked at the return address. Perris. He had to get there. Ky bought a Metro Link ticket for the first train to Perris.

One of the only areas that could out smog Los Angeles was now visible as the train made it's way through the city of Riverside. Entering the Perris Valley the air cleared. Just like the early 90's Ky saw the welcome to the city of Perris sign as his train passed it. The next landmark was the Rock Castle on the hill.

Ky looked up at it as the train went passed. It was a beautiful sight. He imagined owning it. Maybe put a helipad on the roof. His thoughts went back to Linda and his son when the train stopped at the historic Perris Station. Was there a new man? Ky didn't know what to expect.

The 40 minute train ride was nothing compared to the Amtrack trip from Santa Rosa to Los Angeles. The sun was going down. Ky rolled across the street from the Metro Link station to Chicken King. The Asian man behind the counter greeted Ky.

Ky handed the man the envelope with his wife's address on it.

"Do you know where that is?" Ky asked.

"Um, let me see," The Asian man put on his reading glasses. "Oh yeah, 6th Street is two blocks that way!" The man pointed to the south.

"Thank you sir!" Ky pulled out his last two dollars and ordered two slices of Pizza. Despite the name Chicken King, the restaurant served Pizza and Chinese food along with Chicken. A classic ghetto restaurant in the heart of downtown Perris.

Ky was hungry. He devoured both slices. Thirsty, Ky rolled into the restroom. The sink was low. Perfect size for him to cup water in his hands and bring his face forward to drink. Unfortunately the mirror was too high. Ky wiped his mouth with his shirt then rolled out of the restroom to leave Chicken King.

"Have a nice day!" The Asian man behind the counter waved to Ky.

Ky took a deep breath. Free dusty So-Cal air tasted a million times better than the crisp fresh clean air of the Redwoods, which surrounded his former prison.

Ky didn't spend much time in downtown in his previous long ago trips to Perris. He didn't know his way around. The soon to be setting Sun would not help his cause. Ky rolled from the curb to the parking lot to get on his way. He stopped to watch an all white Caprice with tinted windows glide into the Chicken King parking lot with 24" rims. The doors opened and Young Jeezy's Thug Motivation 101 played loudly from the cars sound system. The music muted when the drivers door closed. Standing a slim 6 foot 2 was Pop's. Pop's was a Crip from Compton. He turned his head to look at Ky when he felt the man in the wheelchair staring at him.

Pop's put his left hand on the 357-revolver in his waistband.

The 50 year old Pop's was a known dope dealer. He didn't want
any problems. His mission was to get a bucket of Chicken for
his 20 year old nephew and him to eat for dinner. Every dope
dealer that strayed too far from the safety of the Jay's was
on high alert after a young Watts crip was found shot to death
in the Hazet Market Liquor Store parking lot. Just four blocks
from the Jay's. The rumor was that the local gang's were targeting
the Los Angeles dope dealers.

Pop's wasn't taking any chances. Pop's spun to face the
wheelchaired man slighty lifting his shirt to reveal that he
was armed. "What's up loc,you got a problem?"

Ky was taken aback by the mans brashness, "Naw brotha
I don't want any problems. I just got out of prison. I was admiring
your ride."

Pop's took a good look at Ky,"Is that you homey? Ky?"
Pop's heard the story of how his friend Ky stood up for his 20
year old son in prison. Ky got stabbed in the riot. Pop's owed
Ky everything. But Ky was serving a life sentence. Could this
really be him?

"Pop's?" Ky asked as he rolled closer.

"Oh man Ky, I never thought I would see you again."

"All praise be to Allah! I stayed humble and he freed
me!"

"Ah that's good Ky! Real good!"

"How is you son?" Ky asked.

"Yeah, he told me what you did for him. The knucleheads
in The City (referring to L.A.). Probably locked up again. The
kid can't stay out of jail. I really owe you one! You going to

the Jay's?" Pop's asked.

"No, I'm done with the game brotha. I'm out here to see my son. I just got out today." Ky answered.

"Where's your son at?" Pop's asked.

"6th Street."

"That's only a few blocks away, I'll give you a ride!" Pop's offered.

After Pop's bought his bucket of chicken he helped Ky into the backseat of his white Caprice and loaded his wheelchair into the trunk.

Once on 6th Street Ky handed Pop's the envelope with Linda's address on it. Pop's drove up and down 6th Street three times before he found the address on the envelope. Pop's pulled the wheelchair from his trunk then helped Ky get into it.

"You want me to wait for you?" Pop's asked.

"No. I know my way to the Jay's if nobodies here." It was already dark. Ky was willing to wait outside all night if Linda and Champ weren't home.

"Well here homey take this!" Pop's pulled out his fully loaded 357 hand gun, handing it to Ky.

"I don't need that, I have Allah to protect me!" Ky turned down the offer of Pop's gun.

"Protect you?" Pop's questioned his old friends wisdom, "It's not the same as it used to be Ky. If you are not strapped these kid's around here will leave you naked in the street! Sell you clothes and wheelchair to a pawnshop! You have to take this,

you saved my son's life! This is the least I can do for you,
I owe you more!"

Ky gave in and accepted the gun from Pop's.Ky put the
gun underneath him sitting on it. This was his way of concealing
the weapon.

Before getting into his Caprice to leave Pop's pulled
a roll of twenty hundred dollar bill's from his pocket, handing
it to Ky.

"If you need me you know where I'm at!" Pop's said.

"Thank you Pop's! I'll come to see you when I get settled."
With that Ky was on his own. First night out of prison. Ky rolled
to the door of apartment four and knocked.

After twenty knocks Ky gave up. He rechecked the address.
It was the right place. Not deterred Ky knocked on the neighbors
door. Nobody answered. At apartment two a small hispanic woman
opened her door. Ky showed the woman a picture of Linda and Champ
from 2005.

She shook her head side to side. Ky went to the last door.
Apartment one. He knocked

*

"Get up! Get up!" A bucket of dirty cold water was thrown
onto Champ to wake him.

Champ laid on the floor of a dirty cell. Two masked men
lifted Champ to his feet by his arms. A man in uniform stood
in the cells doorway. It was a Russian man. KGB. The United States
was not the only player in The Horn. Russia sided with Ethiopia

and also secretly with al-Shabaab. After the cold war relations had improved between the KGB and CIA enough for a respectful relationship to develope. Favors would be carried out by the secretive entities when in a position. For instance the KGB had enough influence in the region to gain control of an al-Shabaab prisoner. A top-secret CIA agent named Champ.

"You're lucky!" The KGB member spoke to Champ, "You would be dead if it weren't for me!"

"What,who are you?" Champ questioned the man. Champ was tired, disoriented, wet, cold.

"Just call me God!" The KGB man shined a bright flashlight into Champs eye's as one of the masked men who held Champ up by the arms stuck a syringe into Champs neck.

It's so bright! The gates of Heaven are opening for Champ. "Champ! Champ! Stop climbing over the seats boy! Come give your mother a hug." Linda stood in a beautiful flower printed dress. "Mama!" Champ ran for his mothers arms but she faded with the light!

Champ was in a dark alley. There was a boy. It was the boy Champ encountered on the night of his first battle in Somalia. The little boy he gave the Snickers bar to.

"No, you eat it!" Champ told the boy as he got closer with the snickers bar held in hand as if returning it. "Eat it!" Champ told him as he got even closer.

What first appeared the Snickers bar was a small fanged serpent that rapidly grew large striking forward consuming Champ. He was in darkness!

## Chapter-14

Nine years later-2016

San Bernardino California, Population of Metropolitan Area
5-Million

Five million people would be something if it were not
for the all consuming population of 15-Million people to the
West of San Bernardino.

Los Angeles spawned the larges street gang's in the Nation.
Those gang's spread around the World. Bloods, Crips, 18 Street,
and MS-13. San Bernardino cut from a similar cloth bred the Worlds
largest Outlaw Biker Clubs. The Hell's Angels, Mongals, Vagos.
If Champ could be returned to a city in America that resembled
a war-torn African nation, San Bernardino would be that city.

Brian set Champ up in a low-income apartment in a part
of San Bernardino known as 'Little Africa'. The name comes from
the large percentage of African immigrants that made up the area.

"Champ I have to personally thank you for all that you have done for the Agency. I admire the strength and fortitude you have. You are strong Champ, you were born for this!" Brian sat on a couch opposite Champ in the dimly lit apartment.

Champ was nolonger the innocent kid Brian had first lured into serving as a covert agent in the CIA. He was now a hardened agent, forged from a brutal life of losses. Champ was not in the agency for money, power, or status. It was now 'of him'. He was born for this.

"I'll do what's ever needed Brian, what's next?" After being returned from Africa Champ had spent the past nine years working covertly inside of Patton State Hospital as a Psych Tech.

His nearly decade of work foiled a terrorist plot that would have had nation wide consequences. A group of four Kenyan brothers who worked at the hospital had plans to bring an inferno to the nations traffic jams. It took years of trust building for Champ to be let in on their plans. They planned to use motorcycles to disperse a flammable liquid onto rows of traffic jammed vehicles while following motorbikes had the incinerators. Blowtorches strapped to the back of their bikes.

After Champ foiled the plot he was already asking Brian, "What's next?"

"Whoa, slow down Champ. I just wanted to stop by not only to congratulate you, but also to see how you are holding up? You Okay?"

"Brian I don't need to be checked on! Just tell me what you need me to do and I'll do it. What's next?"

Brian had to accept what he created. "I'll call you!"

*

The year of 2016 was upon the world. Seventy years removed from the last world war nations across the globe had been spun so tight with tension that an explosion was inevitable.

As a nation none was more exposed than Israel. After a failed attack to destroy Iran's nuclear program they braced for a military response. After signing it's nuclear deal with Iran the United States refused to sanction the attack. President Eileen O'Conner publicly stated that the United States would not assist Israel if Iran decided to strike back at them.

The truth was now upon the world. Israel forced the world to take sides. Iran expecting the Israeli attack preemptively moved twelve of it's submarines and six Destroyers to the Mediterranean Sea. Israel's Navy, more sophisticated than the Iranian's yet outnumbered, fired at the Iranian submarines as they sped to close to the Israeli coastline. With only five Destroyers and three submarines making up Israel's small Navy, the country relied upon the Air Force.

The Iranian submarines were easy targets for Israel's bomber planes. Knowing they were easy targets the Iranian submarines began to sink Israel's five Destroyers and three rival submarines.

The skirmish began when the first Iranian submarine was hit. The eleven remaining fired at the same time hitting all three of Israel's submarines, and sinking two Destroyers.

The Israeli bombers dropped a dozen more water penetrating bombs taking out eight more Iranian submarines. In a last ditch effort to accomplish their mission of destroying Israel's naval defenses, the three remaining submarines targeted the last of Israel's Destroyers. All three Israeli Destroyers were hit and began to sink to the ocean floor. When ordered the six Iranian Destroyers would approach the coast and fire missiles at Israeli cities.

On the opposite side of Israel passed it's eastern border, a second skirmish of Israeli and Iranian fighter Jets began a large dogfight. Just one Israeli fighter Jet could shoot down three Iranian fighters with ease. Over five-hundred Jets fought and crashed over the countries of Jordan, and Syria. It looked as if the rapture had started. The explosion's in the sky and land were many.

Iran fired it's long range missiles by the hundred's at Israel. Israel's missile defense system became useless. The entire country of Israel was blanketed by the missiles. Out of desperation Israel confirmed what the world long feared to be true. Five large rockets began launching from the small nation. Five rockets armed with nuclear warheads were headed for five major cities of Iran. Civilian death would be in the million's! Tehran, Mashhad, Esfahan, Shiraz, and Tabriz Iran were all hit with a warhead. Containing over twelve million of Iran's population the cities were targeted to break the will of the Iranian's.

The Europeans agreed with Israel's actions and sent their own militaries to fight off the Iranian's and protect Israel. The Peoples Republic of China sided their nation with Iran. After the nuclear bombing China ordered it's own military to protect Iran. Starting with the largest movement of military aircraft in the history of the world, with over two-thousand Chinese planes bound for Israel.

Tajikistan, Afghanistan, and Pakistan could only watch in awe as the massive air power of China blocked out the Sun as it flew over their nations. China's air superiority was evident with the massive bombing of Israel and destroying of it's Air Force. A European Army led by Germany engaged in the fighting over Israel. A land of only eight-thousand square miles was being fought over by the largest militaries on Earth. China and Iran from the East. Europe and Israel from the West. Other nations could only hope to avoid becoming part of World War Three. One of these nations being the United States of America.

*

President Eileen O'Conner felt her sanity slipping away
more and more with every passing day. Not only was the first
female United States President fighting for her political life,
she was also tasked with keeping the nation from war. One important
step was distancing the country from the North Atlantic Treaty
organization (NATO), and Israel. In the Oval Office of the White
House President O'Conner spoke to her puppet master. The Head
of the Central Intelligence Agency. Samuel R. Richerdson. Two
of only a selective few who know about the United States strategically
placed nuclear rockets. Buried in the valleys of Afghanistan
were hundreds of missile silo's secretly operated by the United
States. If needed the entire countries of China, Russia, or Iran
could be bombed in under ten minutes!

"Samuel I don't know what I'm doing anymore? I can't make
decisions, my mind is cluttered with so many thoughts of what
one mistake could cause." President O'Conner sat at her desk
speaking to Samuel.

"Just stand your ground publicly. You need to be a firm
voice for the nation. There is no need to rush into this war.
The public would turn against us if we did that. Then that Mexican
would get in here and put our whole nation in jeopardy." Samuel
was respected by everybody in the intelligence community, even
most of Congress. The rare exception being Senator Juan Carlos.
The young Democratic stud was ahead in popular opinion polls.
Projected to become the forty-sixth President of the United States,
Samuel knew if Carlos got into office he himself would lose power.
As of now he had control of a gullible President who needed him.
Samuel craved the power. Making back up plans Samuel spoke to
Senator Carlos's running mate. If worse came to worse he would
still have a hand in the door.

"What do we do about Taiwan?" The President asked Samuel.

China wasted no time in seizing the Island once fighting began. The United States being responsible for much of Taiwan's security lost an Aircraft Carrier in the battle for the Island of twenty-three million. The United States ordered what was left of the carrier group to the Sea of Japan to bolster security around Japan, and South Korea. Taiwan's two million man military could not hold against the ten million chinese soldiers sent to occupy the Island.

"We accept it! Inform China we don't want a war. When every tear drop is a waterfall here at home is when we go to war. China won't know what to do when all their cities are burning." Samuel told the President.

"I'm sorry I let you down Samuel, but I am done. I can't take this shit! Have the Veep do this!" President O'Conner was mentally broken down. All she wanted was to get away. Get her mind right. The problem with that is it was Tuesday November 8th 2016. Election Day. President Eileen O'Conner retreated to her West Coast White House in Orange County California to hide from the world.

*

Senator Juan Carlos won in a land slide victory! With the absence of the current president and refusal of Vice President to fulfill his duties, Congress enacted an emergency stature allowing Senator Juan Carlos to be sworn into office early. On a visit to China President Juan Carlos worked out a peace plan with the communist government. Signing a non-aggression treaty assured that the United States could avoid the war raging on across Asia, and Europe.

Samuel Richerdson was furious by the Presidents actions. How could he let the Chinese get away with their bombing of European cities! The Chinese bombing was mainly in Germany, France, Italy, and Spain. Samuel contacted his Russian contacts to activate their joint opperations that was years in the making. From the remote border of Ethiopia-Somalia, the Chinese made gas bombs were launched on ballistic milliles. The Russian's built this facility and ballistic missiles for the purpose of striking American cities. The Chinese would be blamed. Thus prompting an American response so vicious the Earth may be knocked out of orbit!

Samuel expected to be hailed as a hero after he would pubicly order the annihilation of China. Bringing about the end of World War Three. Samuel would then declare himself the Messiah! His goal was to create a one world government. The nations who choose not to fall in line would be considered an evil empire and taken by force! Since birth Samuel fantasised about this moment. The moment he ran the world! Samuel believed that the world spun for him!

\*

Eleven year old Jackson left his Riverside California home with only a backpack. He carried a plane ticket. Jackson was different from other kid's. His Grandmother took him to different doctors, but all had the same diagnosis. Autism. His entire life he never spoke. His Grandmother realized by the time Jackson was eight years old that he liked to read. History books seemed to keep his attention the longest. Every year Jackson would watch Dick Clarks Rockin New Years Eve. He stared at the screen for hours. Often staying up watching to the early morning. This year would be no different Colleen thought. She was asleep in her room when Jackson left the house.

Jackson rode a city bus to the Ontario International Airport. He had a plane ticket. Nobody stopped the eleven year old boy from boarding the flight to New York City.

\*

Brian Benson knew how much Samuel disliked President Carlos. He needed an agent he could trust to look for anything fishy.

Champ boarded a secret service helicopter. The President was about to start giving his speach to the nation.

Brian sat at his desk at The Hotel viewing the Trump Card over Salt Lake City.

"Excuse me Agent Benson, we're going to need you to come with us!" A deep voice spoke from behind him.

Brian stood to face two Agents who wore suits and sunglasses like the Men in Black. Brian pulled his gun and shot both men before they could react! Brian knew Samuel was up to something, that's why the two agents were sent to arrest him. He had to warn Champ! Samuel knew Champ was with the secret service in the helicopter. Champ was in danger!

Brian quickly left The Hotel. Walking to his car he pulled out his cell phone to call Champ. There was not enough time. Agents exited two black vans and shot Brian to death with over a hundred bullets from Automatic Rifles. His body was quickly rolled into a bag and loaded into one of the black vans.

The lead Agent picked up Brian's cell phone and looked at the last number dialed. It was to Champ. The Agent called Samuel.

"Benson was K.I.A.. His last call was to Champ Washington." The agent said.

"Is Washington still in the helicopter?" Samuel asked.

"Yes sir! He didn't have enough time to warn him." The agent answered.

"Is the rifle in place?" Asked Samuel.

"Confirmed!" Agent responded.

President Juan Carlos took to the podium to give his speech. Champ watched him from above from the secret service helicopter.

"My fellow Americans. As we approach the new year in a few short minutes, we have a historic year ahead of us. We are no longer going to be the police of the world. Today's world is too small for us and those other powers that wish to see us fail as a nation. The United States interest no longer exist ouside of our shores. It's time for us to do our nation building in our own nation. Skid Row needs hope, the 9th ward needs to float, and the South Side of Chicago needs to be the best side of Chicago! I will..." Samuel Richerdson had heard enough. He used Ghost to slay the man that stood between him and absolute power.

Champ watched with the nation the Presidents live assassination. Thoughts of how his mothers head exploded quickly came to his mind, and was the last thought he took with him to unconsciousness. Champ had been shot with a tranquilizer by one of Samuel's agents who was also aboard the helicopter.

*

Eleven year old Jackson's Grandmother Colleen had driven around her Riverside California neighborhood for hours looking for her grandson. She only returned home after she heard on her car's radio about the assassination of the boy's father. Her son-in-law. President Juan Carlos. Colleen tried unsuccessfully to reach her daughter, the First Lady. The news of the Presidents assassination was interrupted by a massive attack taking place against the United States. Colleen watched her television in horror as the live broadcast from Times Square showed the gassing of the city. A pile of five million dead Americans was shown live across the entire world.

The still image of desperation was interrupted by movement. A young boy could be seen running through the sea of death. All watched this boy. He approached a live camera. Picking up a microphone from a dead hosts hand. Colleen thought she would faint! It was Jackson! Her Jackson! The boy who never spoke a word in his life had the attention of the world. And he spoke!

"This sea of death will bring life. Since I was born I knew what my purpose in life is. To be here at this very moment. To speak to you. The world. We can nolonger murder each other! I am here to bring the peace. Do not reject me!" The media replayed the video over and over again dubbing it the Miracle Boy footage! The last the world saw of the boy was the black helicopter that landed on top of bodies. Men in haz-mat suits snatched the boy from in front of the camera and flew away with him.

From his office in Langley Virginia (CIA Headquarters) Samuel's plan was working. He ordered launched over one-hundred nuclear warheads to destroy China. The Miracle Boy was  nexpected. Nobody could survive the poison gas. There was something extremely special about this boy. Samuel sent a team to retrieve the boy and bring him back to Langley.

## Chapter-15

The lights were bright! It was hard for Champ to see. Had he been drugged? He didn't know? With blury vision Champ could make out a wide blue door. He wobbled his way to the door and tried to push it open. It was solid. No handle. It was a cell door! He was in prison! Champs head throbbed. He got dizzy and hit the floor unconscious.

"Hey! Thirty-nine do you hear me? Number thirty-nine wake up! It's breakfast time. Are you going to eat?" The female nurse removed her finger from holding open Champs eye and put the flash light away. "He's not responsive." The nurse told the guard who accompanied her to number thirty-nine's cell.

"Alright we'll get a gurney. Roll him to medical." The lead guard said. Champ was taken to medical where an I.V. had been inserted into his arm. Inmate thirty-nine was a new arrival at the top secret CIA prison. The lead nurse at the prison was recruited by the CIA fresh out of college. Never married and mother of a ten year old boy, the twenty-seven year old was perfect for her job.

The only thing she knew about her patients was their age, race, and number. She continued trying to wake number thirty-nine. "Thirty-nine wake up! Thirty-nine!" Knowing if a patient slipped into a coma they would most likely die due to the limited medical attention provided to the inmates of the secret prison. The nurse cared about the survival of her patients. She may have not been able to get them out of prison but she was able to at least keep them alive.

"Owww! Champ yelled like a wounded beast when he opened his eye's. Not in pain but frustration by the straps holding him down to the gurney. "They killed my mother! Mama! Mama!" Champ screamed from the top of his lungs.

Number thirty-nine was in shock and the nurse had no choice but to sedate him. Champ slowly retreated back into unconsciousness. "Well there is nothing I can do for him. You can take him back to his cell." The nurse told the guard. She felt bad but what could she do about it? She worked for the CIA.

The nurse left the secret CIA prison. Her day was done. She exited the prison known as The Hotel. She got into her vehicle, she always parked on A Street.

She drove a few blocks to 3rd Street were she turned right and pulled into the parking lot of Chicken King. She would bring her ten year old pizza home for dinner.

The 54 year old Ky saw the woman pull into the parking lot. He still had hopes of finding out what happened to his son? After 9 years he still questioned customers of Chicken King if they knew what happened to his boy? The lady almost got into the restaurant trying to ignore him. He shoved the picture of Linda and Champ in front of the nurse.

"Oh my God sir! What is your broblem?" The nurse questioned Ky.

"The boy, he's my son. He's missing, please look at him!" Ky gave the nurse the picture.

Sofia had not seen Champ like that since the 8th grade. He had the face of his son. Sofia still remembered that night on the roof in Provo Utah. 'I will see you again' Champ told her. he was still waiting for the day. A year after Champ disappeared to Somalia, Sofia was propositioned by an agent to work as for the CIA. Agent Brian Benson approached Sofia three months after she gave birth to Champs baby.

"You said this is your son?" Sofia questioned.

"Yeah. My boy. Do you know him?" Ky was hopeful this girl could tell him something.

"I did know Champ but I haven't seen him in ten years." Sofia did not fully trust this man but then again he could be her son's grandfather? That is of course if this was really Champs father?

"Yeah! Champ! That's my boy! Please I need to find him! Tell me anything you know about him? I'll pay you?" Ky pulled a handful of crumpled hundred dollar bills from his pocket.

"No, it's fine sir. I don't need your money. But honestly I don't know how I can help you find Champ. I haven't seen him in ten years!"

"Well what happened to him, where did he go?" Ky asked.

"Last time I saw him was in Utah. He was going overseas." Sofia remebered Champ telling her how the CIA promised to get his father out of prison if he went on the mission for them.

Obviously his father didn't know what Champ did for him.

"Overseas? I don't understand? He was in juvenlie hall, his mother was murdered, what was he doing in Utah?" Ky was thoroughly confused.

"You really don't know anything about what Champ did for you?" Sofia asked.

Ky shed a tear. "No. I don't know what happened to my son?"

"Would you like to go inside? I have some information that might be able to help you."

The two went to a booth inside of Chicken King.

After Sofia explained the deal Champ had made with the CIA Ky was satisfied yet disturbed with the knowledge. Sofia began to ask Ky about himself. How was he enjoying his freedom, despite the state of the nation?

Ky watched with everybody the live assassination of the President. The United States was preparing for an all out war with China. Los Angeles and San Diego were hit by the gas bombs causing a massive influx of people to flee inland. They hoped to avoid being the victim of a nuclear warhead. China denied attacking the United States but the head of the CIA was certain it was them. He planned a nuclear response within 24-hours. First Samuel Richerdson was due in front of congress to explain what happened and what actions would be necessary to secure the safety of our nation.

The city of Perris had it's population double over night after the attack. The hotel and motel's of the city were sold-out. The Perris Valley Airport had been transformed into a refugee camp. Few had tents, others slept in their vehicles.

"I thought there was nothing in life worse than having life in prison, yet now the country is in world war three and my son is in the CIA." Ky had his head in his hands.

"I'm, a grandfather! When can I see my grandson?" Ky asked.

Sofia remebered she had to get home to her son. "Maybe tomorrow, will you be here around this time?" Sofia got up to leave with a box of pizza for her son in her hands.

"Yes I will be, I'm here everday!" Ky said with a bright smile.

Sofia arrived home to her affluent Perris neighborhood called May Ranch. The ten year old Champ Jr. smiled as he greeted his mother at the front door of their two story track home. Sofia always thought of how much Champ Jr. looked like his father when he smiled at her. Champ was often on her mind. And now she met his father. How strange was that she thought? Before Sofia entered her house she saw number thirty-nine (her patient from work) in her mind. The way he snapped out of consciousness with eye's as bright as her son's. Champ!

Sofia handed her son the pizza and raced back to her car. The babysitter appeared in the doorway and called after her, "Sofia I can't stay! I have school tomorrow!"

"Please I need this favor! I will pay you double!" Sofia yelled back to her.

The babysitter was fine with those terms. Sofia was off driving back to Chicken King.

Ky watched Sofia's car pull back into the chicken King

parking lot. "I know where Champ is!" Sofia said as she hurried from her car.

"Where is he?" Ky questioned.

"At my work. He's a patient, uh prisoner. What is he doing there?" Sofia spoke in a hurried panic.

"Where do you work?" Ky questioned Sofia.

Sofia turned to the Rock Castle that sat on a hill above the city. She pointed at it, "I work inside of there. Under the Rock Castle is a prison. Nobody knows about it. It's top secret. CIA."

Ky looked at the Rock Castle then back at Sofia. "Are you okay?"

"Am I okay? No I'm not okay! Champ is in there and he's hurting! We have to get him out!"

"Wait a minute and calm down. If what you are saying is true I'll roll over there myself to rescue my son. I am just having a hard time wrapping my mind around what you are saying to me right now."

Sofia pulled out her security clearance card. "This is what I show the guards to gain access. I have to walk through a body scanner when I enter or leave."

Ky took a hard look at Sofia's security clearance card. "CIA level-2. Are you in the CIA?"

"No no I am just a nurse. I take care of the prisoners. I am not told their names, just the numbers they are given. Thirty-nin

"Thirty-nine?"

"Thirty-nine is Champs number. I didn't recognize him.
He is in bad shape. He's face is swollen. When I got home to
see Champ Jr. his eye's gave it away. It's Champ. Prisoner thirty-nine
is Champ. He's in there." Sofia once again looked over to what
was known to the CIA as The Hotel.

"Let me use your phone!" Ky believed everything Sofia
was saying. Why would she have driven back to Chicken King to
tell Ky of a wild fantasy.

"Who are you calling?" Sofia asked while handing Ky her
phone.

"A friend. He might be able to help us."

*

A three car motorcade pulled into the parking lot of Chicken
King. Led by Pop's all white Caprice. Two large all black S.U.V.'s
trailed. The bass from the vehicle's sound systems vibrated thorugh
the pavement. The crew Pop's brought with him was heavily armed
with M-16's. Ski mask sat on their heads folded as beenies. Bullet
proof vest served as their protection. Ky was handed an M-16
by Pop's. This would be for Champ. Sofia would lead the way to
the secret entrance from A Street at the rear of the Rock Castle.

"You're back out of schedule." The sentry commented to
Sofia as she gained access with her security clearence card.

"So busy I forgot to log off of my computer." Sofia quickly
responded, walking briskly to her work space with her ultimate
goal of getting to patient thirty-nine.

Ky rolled his wheelchair to what appeared from a distance
to be a plain large boulder. Up close Ky could see the lines

that allowed the boulders face to slide down into the hillside revealing the top secret entrance.

"Crack! Crack! Crack!" The sound of Ky's M-16 chipping away at the boulder faced door could be heard throughout The Hotel. Startled agents rushed around trying to grasp what was happening. Security cameras hidden from view of outsiders allowed the sentry to view the man in the wheelchair letting off rounds at the door.

"Come on you motherfuckers! Open that bitch up!" Ky yelled at the boulder.

"What do you want me to do?" The sentry asked his superior who now stood next to him also viewing Ky.

"Get rid of that guy before a civilian spot's him."

Ky aimed the M-16 at the door. The M-16 caused Ky to roll backwards as he fired. He didn't have great mobility. Ky snapped his brakes on taking a stern firing position on the door. "Come on you bitchs!" Ky yelled at the boulder.

With great speed the boulder slid away with a great burst of light shooting from the darkened entrance to The Hotel. Three agents fired simultaneously into Ky's body. Ky was thrown three feet backwards out of his wheelchair. Ky lie on his back staring at the sky.

"Yard down! Yard down!" Blared away inside of Ky's mind. He was transported back to Pelican Bay's B-yard. "Fucking Mexicans finally got me." Were Ky's last thoughts as his spirit shifted into the darkness.

The three CIA agents stepped from the safety of The Hotel. They failed to notice the ten ski-masked men strategically spaced out hiding behind different boulders. Pop's crew open fire quickly

downing the three agents. Pop's leap down from above and behind
the secret door. With 357 in hand and blue rag around his face
Pop's led his crew into The Hotel.

Sofia stared at Champ who lie face in drool. She jingled
the keys loudly against the cell door as she unlocked it, "Champ
wake up! Champ!" Sofia squeezed Champs shoulders.

Champ slowly opened his eye's to catch those of Sofia's.
His first words came out as a mumble. "Ah um whatcha whata whoa
whoe Sofia!" Champ recognized her. Recognized Sofia's pure beauty.
Body and spirit. Champ was infused with a bliss that helped him
rise to his feet. "Sofia what are you doing here?"

"I came to free you, let's go!" Sofia grabbed Champs hand
and attempted to lead him off.

Champ pulled her back towards him. Champ looked Sofia
in the eye's with a smile, "Sofia!"

"Yeah?" Sofia felt the power of this man.

"Told you I would see you again!"

Sofia led Champ through the hall's of The Hotel towards
the exit. A fire fight could be heard in the distance.

"Pow! Pow!" Two shots from an agent's Glock flew over
Sofia and Champs head. Champs swung Sofia behind a desk. With
a dip of his shoulder Champ came up grabbing the agent. "Pow!"
the gun went off next to Champs ear. Missing him. Champ slung
the agent to the floor with such force it broke the agents back
and knocked him unconscious.

"Sofia let's go!" Champ picked up the agents gun.

"Wait Champ! I brought your father to help us. He and

his friends are shooting it out with the agents."

"My fathers dead. He died in prison Sofia. Who did you bring with you?" Champ instantly feared who had come to get him.

"No Champ. He really is you father. He's in a wheelchair. Your dad survived prison."

"Stay behind me Sofia. You were set up to get me killed. My fathers dead." Champ was sure of himself.

"No Champ you're wrong." Sofia didn't know what to beleive. Was she deceived?

Pop's crew had taken several causality's. They receded back towards the entrance of The Hotel by order of Pop's. He proceeded forward knocking off the two remaining agents in his way.

"Pow!" Champ shot Pop's in the head as he failed to check a corner

"No!" Sofia yelled at Champ. "These are your friends! They came to help you!"

Champ grabbed Sofia by the arms and sternly told her, "Nobodies my friend! Everybody wants to kill me!"

"I can't go with you Champ." Sofia collapsed down looking up at Champ through teary eye's. "Go Champ, take my car." Sofia handed Champ her car keys.

Champ looked down at Sofia while taking her car key's. "I love you!"

Champ exited The Hotel and ran into two O.G.'s from Pop's crew. The rest of Pop's crew retreated to the black S.U.V.'s

with their fallen soldiers. Champ shot both of them as they held
their M-16's at their side. Champ ran to Sofia's car not thinking
twice about the bloodied man next to an empty wheelchair. He
simply ran passed the man. Champ was in survival mode.

The only resonably safe place Champ could go was to an
apartment in Moreno Valley that served as one of Brian's safe
houses.

Champ closed all blinds sitting in the darkness of the
apartment. A secure cell phone sat on the coffee table next to
the Glock in front of Champ. He had been unable to reach Brian.
Champ would eat and get some sleep through the uneasy night.
He would leave the apartment in the morning. Didn't know where
he would go but was sure like  it always had; trouble would find
him.

\*

Tiny Duke and Pitbull had trailed Champ from the Rock
Castle to the apartment in Moreno Valley. They waited on word
from their bigger homies in San Bernardino on what to do. A morning
meeting of O.G.'s determined Champ had to be killed for deading
Pop's. He would serve the same fate as the girl. Sofia's body
had already been sunken to the depths of Perris Lake

A Predator drone was ascending from the runway at the March
Air Reserve Base. From the drones high definition camera two
Inland Empire gang members could be seen walking up the steps
towards the apartment Champ was in. Their gang affiliation was
made clear by the visible I.E. tattoos on their neck and forearms.

Champ was woken by the sound of banging on the apartment
door. Jumping from the couch Champ grabbed the Glock from the
table and pointed it at the door.

The explosion was incredible. The entire apartment shook as the Predator drone unleashed a volley of fire through the M-16 toting gangster's. The apartment door along with half of the front wall of the apartment was ripped to shreds. Champ was thrown to the carpet by the force. Restanding Champ grabbed the cell phone and car key's that also fell and strode from the apartment not failing to pick up an M-16 from one of the fallen gnagster's.

    A neighbor spooked by the chaos dialed in to 911,"A man with a big gun is shooting people! Help! Hurry!"

## Chapter-16

"Dispatch I have an eye on suspects vehicle. Traveling west on Alassandro. I'm going to light him up." The Riverside County Sheriffs Deputy turned on his lights and sirens. "Dispatch, suspect is failure to yield. Initiate pursuit protocol. I need a bird in the air."

Champ saw the deputies lights. It didn't matter. Champ had been placed in one too many cages in his life time. He was not going to allow a Sheriffs Deputy to re-chain him. Champ entered the 215 freeway.

"Dispatch suspect is merging. 215 north now 60 west. Where is my bird!" The lone Sheriffs Deputy radioed into dispatch.

Champ briefly crossed from Riverside into San Bernardino County. From San Bernardino County Champ sped into Los Angeles. The Highway Patrol took over pursuit duties from the Riverside County Sheriffs Deputy. "I wanted to shoot the prick so bad."

Mumbled the Deputy as he returned to his County.

The west bound traffic was sparse. Most citizens were moving inland trying to avoid becoming the victim of foreign military aggression.

The cell phone that sat next to Champ on the passenger seat began to ring. Champ answered it hoping that it was Brian. "Hello!"

"Champ head to the U.S. Bank Tower downtown! I have a chopper waiting for you on the roof. It will bring you to safety." Samuel ended the call. Champ did not recognize the caller's voice. "Who are you?" Champ looked at the phone. The line was dead.

A L.A.P.D. helicopter joined in on the high speed chase. "I have a visual on suspects vehicle. He is heading downtown. Stupid bastards going to corner himself. Won't have anywhere to go."

Champ stopped his vehicle at 633 W. 5th St. The U.S. Bank Tower rose 1,018 feet in front of him. He would have to cover 73-stories to reach the helicopter on the roof.

"Suspect ran into the bank tower! Repeat suspect ran into bank tower! There is a black copter on the helipad! Repeat do not let suspect reach that helicopter damn it!" The L.A.P.D. helicopter pilot radioed.

The U.S. Bank Tower has stood as the tallest building west of the mississippi since it was constructed in 1990. The Wilshire Grand Tower currently under construction downtown was set to steal that distinction. For now this was the tallest perch in the city. Champ reached the blacked out helicopter in full sweat, out of breath.

"Don't you enter that copter scum bag!" Came from a loud

speaker on the L.A.P.D. helicopter.

Champ flipped him the middle finger before getting into the black helicopter. The pilot of Champs getaway bird was a veteran. He purposely flew over L.A.X. restricted airspace where the L.A.P.D. helicopter pilot would not dare follow.

"Where are we going?" Champ asked the pilot as they flew out over the Pacific Ocean.

"Channel Islands. Samuel needs to see you."

\*

Channel Islands

The rocket was in launch position. It carried not a nuclear warhead atop. A CIA space shuttle would rely upon the rockets lift. Samuel would blast off to a top secret Moon base on the dark side of the Moon. The base was construted shortly after the first Moon landings some time in the 60's. Samuel did not want to stick around the Planet. The Earth was getting ready to experience a mass die off of it's native population. The pending nuclear volley between America, China, and Russia would cause a massive nuclear annihilation of life on Earth. Only those lucky few underground, or in outer space could survive. Of course there were those two special beings samuel had discovered. The Boy. Jackson. And the other? A woman. 25 year old Marissa. Samuel had her picked up from her horse ranch in Montana. Samuel would stash the pair inside of a deep underground bunker on the Islands. Champ would join them. Samuel would need them if humanity hoped of ever reclaiming the Earth for Humans. The question had been answered long ago for those of us who had already become enlightened. We were never alone!

The Watchers, Grays, Ant People. All real! But they were nothing for humanity to fear. Humanity had only itself. And okay maybe the Dark Matter Beings should be feared! After all they are the stuff that ghost are made of, thriving on the rejected souls of those not allowed into Heaven. With a mass die off Dark Matter will consume the billons of souls left behind.

The Watchers and Grays will have to fight to keep the Planet from Dark Matter. No light can exist in Dark Matter. If all Consumed by Dark Matter the Earth would collapse into a Black Hole, taking with it neighboring Solar Systems. Home Planets of the Alian Beings would be lost.

The battle for Earth would have to began. This would not be a battle between Humans, or by Humans. They were taking themselves out of the equation.

Samuel escorted Champ into the depths of the underground bunker. Jackson and Marissa greeted Champ as if they had already knew him. Samuel had already told them enough about him.

"What is this?" Champ questioned.

"Take a seat. You're going to need to listen very carefully." Samuel briefed the trio on what would be needed of them. Hope for a home Planet for human beings would depend upon them.

*

Samuel looked at the burning Earth as his space shuttle took him out of the Earth's atmosphere. He tought of a promise God made to humanity written in the Bible;

Genesis 9:11
"Thus I establish my covenant with you: Never again shall all flesh be cut off by the waters of the flood; never

again shall there be a flood to destroy the Earth."

'This time it will be done by fire.' Samuel thought.

There cannot Be a World without Jesus,
    In His Words there Is a World of Hope!
                -Author

## SOMALIA!

As a new author of fiction I mixed reality with it to tackle a tuff subject. I took a well fed struggling teen from an American ghetto and implanted him in one of the most volatile regions on the Earth. The Horn of Africa. The planet is already aware of the women and children that suffer from famine and war in Somalia. I cannot bring the situation to light more than it already is. I just want my readers to think about our brothers and sisters who struggle for life daily while most of us fortunate by birthplace Americans only struggle for wants. If you are not able to physically help the less fortunate at least say a prayer for them. Like air just because you can't see it doesn't mean it's not there. What you do for others matters!